D1123217

1/12

ONE GIRL
COOKIES

grandma connie & grandaddy,
1929, mt. washington, new hampshire

ONE GIRL COOKIES

RECIPES for CAKES, CUPCAKES, WHOOPIE PIES, and COOKIES

from Brooklyn's Beloved Bakery

Dawn Casale & David Crofton

Clarkson Potter/Publishers
New York

For our families, who have taught
us the joys of the table . . .

And for Nate, who will
soon learn them too

Copyright © 2012 by One Girl Cookies Ltd.
Photographs copyright © 2012 by Iain Bagwell

All rights reserved.
Published in the United States by Clarkson Potter/Publishers,
an imprint of the Crown Publishing Group, a division of
Random House, Inc., New York.
www.crownpublishing.com
www.clarksonpotter.com

CLARKSON POTTER is a trademark and POTTER with
colophon is a registered trademark of Random House, Inc.

Library of Congress Cataloging-in-Publication Data
Casale, Dawn.
    One girl cookies / Dawn Casale and David Crofton. — 1st ed.
      p.   cm.
    Includes index.
    1. Cookies.   2. Desserts.   I. Crofton, David.   II. Title.
    TX772.C3822   2012
    641.8'654—dc22   2011008911

ISBN 978-0-307-72048-1

Printed in China

Design by Rae Ann Spitzenberger

10 9 8 7 6 5 4 3 2 1

First Edition

Contents

OUR STORY

Some would call it a love story. We like to think of it as an alignment of the stars and just something that was meant to be. It goes like this . . .

As cliché as it may sound, I was destined to make a living in the world of food—even though I started my career in fashion. I have witnessed firsthand my entire life how food can bring great joy to both the cook and the eater. The joys of sharing a table together have always been clear to me but in a somewhat subconscious way. I just took for granted that all families were like mine. It took my going out into the big city of New York, getting a job in fashion retail, and meeting people from all walks of life to realize that this just wasn't the case. And it finally dawned on me that I wanted to share my love of food with others for a living.

I will begin by saying that I come from a Sicilian family. For some people, that might be enough said. But for those who don't know a family like mine, it would suffice to say that just about every meal is a feast. I do not lie when I say that my lunchbox contained courses. Or that our after-noon snack was often lemony madeleines straight from the oven, almost too hot to touch. And it is also true that my mother is an extraordinary cook and hostess, and her mother—my grandmother Nana—was the same. So I learned what I know about food through osmosis. My fondest memories involve family parties and all of the traditional foods we shared.

So after several years of peddling pretty baubles as the accessories manager at Barneys New York, I had "the moment." The lightbulb lit up, the sirens sounded, and I was ready. Fueled by encouragement from friends and family, I started One Girl Cookies. I was ready to venture down a path paved with butter and flour and sugar, and I had never been happier.

I called it "One Girl" because that's exactly what it was. Me. Moi. Mixing it, baking it, packing it, delivering it. The "it" being pretty little cookies. I had been so used to working with pretty little things that I couldn't imagine doing it any differently. Small, because, who needs more? Big desserts are such a commitment. To me, it was so much better to flirt with all kinds of flavors. A chocolate cookie first. A nutty one next. Followed by a bit of fruit. Who says you can't have it all? Rubbish.

I tested, tried, and tasted all kinds of yummy things. Some were my own creations and others family recipes passed down through several generations of Sicilians. I was in nirvana. I spent every moment of every day mixing, folding, rolling, cutting, and baking. I quickly remembered that very unique smell of butter and sugar being creamed together. I delighted in stirring bubbling caramel until my arm grew numb. I became giddy each time I plunged my hands into the velvety dough, took hold of the pin, and began rolling. And I finished each day eager to fill my building's hallways with the heady aromas of freshly baked cookies all over again.

The cookies and I had developed such an intimate relationship that it just seemed plain wrong to not give them a proper name. And so I did. Lucia, Lana, Penelope, Miranda, Susanna, and Juliette were born to bring happiness into the world. Lucia, named in honor of my great-grandmother, was a layer bar comprised of buttery shortbread, espresso-spiked homemade caramel, and swirls of bittersweet and white chocolates—not just another pretty face, undeniably decadent as well. The spiciest of the bunch—with candied and powdered ginger plus cinnamon and nutmeg—had a natural, no-frills way about it, so the moniker Susanna seemed most fitting.

Since Barneys had been my training ground for how to make things look aesthetically pleasing, the way I was packaging my treats was no less important to me than how they tasted. My idea was to create something that was a tribute, an homage of some sort, to my family, who taught me that food is far more than nourishment for the body. Food feeds the soul. And a well-fed soul is a happy soul. Beyond that, a meal is a way to share time together. And no meal could be deemed delicious unless an outpouring of love was involved in creating it. As a result, foods steeped in tradition were, and still are, a big part of what we eat when we are together. For Christmas Eve, seven fishes are served, representing the seven sacraments. I look forward to the celebration all year because seafood would be my choice for a last supper, and Christmas Eve is the All Star Game for shrimp, mussels, squid, and other creatures from the sea. For Easter, sweet and creamy grain pie and a panettone-like bread embedded with colored hard-boiled eggs is served for dessert. I don't think anyone questions these menu choices, because they are not really choices. It's the way it's been done for generations and these dishes are as much a part of their respective

holidays as Santa and the Easter Bunny are. My personal history has been filled with traditions like this, and my life would never be the same without them. For reasons like this, my relationships with my family and with food are so intertwined. What better way to recognize that than by adorning my boxes of cookies with photos of them?

The photographs themselves tell a story. One is of my paternal grandmother (Nanny) and her sister. They are in their late twenties and clearly ready for a special occasion, decked out in fancy hats, coats, and red lipstick. One of my favorites is an ironic one of my maternal grandmother, Nana, always a jokester, peering very sternly out the window of their Brooklyn apartment. The appeal is that these photographs could just as easily tell someone else's story. My customers saw their own family on the boxes and the cookies that filled them were reminiscent of the Christmas cookie platter they shared at their gathering.

When the first holiday season approached, it became apparent that "one girl" better get another girl, plus a bunch of friends and family and anyone else willing to lend a helping hand. My mom and sisters baked cookies, my aunt and her friend packed boxes, my cousin made deliveries, and each night my roommate reassured me that I would get it all done. Thankfully, I did. When January rolled around, I had two realizations: It truly takes a village to raise a business, and it was time for One Girl to find a new home with room to grow. Little did I know that I was about to embark on a series of fortunate events.

To continue growing, I needed to hire someone who had been formally trained as a baker. Because I had been "home schooled" in baking, there was certain knowledge—particularly about production baking—that I simply did not possess. I put out the word that I was hiring, and a friend mentioned that she worked with a guy who was finishing up pastry school. He happened to be in search of an apartment as well and, coincidentally, my roommate had just moved out. Dave Crofton and I hit it off immediately. We talked about his position at One Girl, and then about sharing an apartment. (Coincidence #2: the apartment that he was vacating was less than half a block away from my apartment. Hmmm.) We both felt that living and working together might prove to be, shall we say, intense. Since he needed a job more than a place to live, and I needed a baker more than a roommate, he reported for work the very next day and continued his search for a new pad.

Things went extraordinarily well. Not only was Dave a talented baker and hard worker, we got along like two old friends. We worked really well as a team and we enjoyed each other's company (perhaps a bit too much), which was a good thing, because we spent an inordinate amount of time together. Dave and I worked side by side for hours, often had dinner together after a long day, and made lots of time for flirting. He was a dream employee for me, and he claims that I was the best boss he'd ever had. Plus, I really liked him. I mean, "liked" him. But much to my dismay, he decided to give something new a try and off he went, with my blessings, into the big bad world of restaurant kitchens. We chatted almost daily about all the goings-on at One Girl and he filled me in on the things he was learning in his new position. But as luck would have it, he ended up not really enjoying his job. He called, groveled a bit, and I took him back, without a teaspoon of hesitation.

We immediately began to discuss the future of One Girl Cookies and all of the greatness we hoped to achieve. We had aspirations of filling the city with happy, cookie-eating people. After a few months, we reconsidered our decision to live in separate apartments. Who says intense is a bad thing? We found a place in Brooklyn and moved in together. That is where I learned of Dave's own big plans. One night, Dave was busily preparing dinner and I was about to hop into the shower when he asked me to check on something in the oven. Now? When I'm wrapped in a towel? OK, I guess. Seemed sort of strange, but I opened the oven door and there, arranged on a baking sheet, were sugar cookies that spelled out "Will you marry me?" I promptly slammed the door shut and broke into a hysterical bout of laughter. Perhaps not the romantic reaction he had expected, but I was simply giddy.

As we planned our wedding, we also planned the opening of our cookie shop. We knew that the right neighborhood was the one we lived in—Cobble Hill, Brooklyn. We searched for just the right shop that would fit the personality of the cookies. Big enough, but not too big. Plus sweet and lovely and pretty. We knew our place was "the one" the second

we saw it. It is situated on a quaint tree-lined street, just off the main thoroughfare, and is perfect in every way. We spent the next several months planning, researching, looking through books, and thinking of every detail imaginable. After three months of construction; the purchase of lots of aqua-blue plates, cups and saucers, milk-glass cake stands, and all sorts of kitchen equipment; plus the selection of just the right play list; the hiring of a friendly, eager staff; and hanging our simple cookies sign outside our storefront, we were open for business. The excitement was overwhelming.

We have since become part of a true community, one that I have often referred to as "Urban Mayberry." It has the charm of a small town, where neighbors greet one another, inquire about families, and lend a helping hand. An oddity for many parts of New York City, but not here. Add to that dynamic energy, diversity, and lots of fellow entrepreneurs, and you've got the perfect place to set up shop. Each time the old-fashioned bell on the door goes ring-a-ling, we are reminded that we have the best jobs in the world.

And until recently, we really did think we had it all. Until it occurred to us that only a very small population of the world knew our story and could enjoy our treats. We think it's a great and fortunate tale and we're delighted to tell it. So, in your hands you hold our story and all of the yummy things that have filled our life and many other lives with delight. Hopefully, as you turn the pages and make the recipes, you will be reminded of your own sweet, lucky story as well.

Comfort Cookies

lauren, robyn & wendy, 1965, dobbs ferry, new york

OLD-FASHIONED GRAHAM CRACKERS WITH TURBINADO SUGAR 14

SPICED GINGER OATMEAL DROPS 15

ORANGE BUTTER DROPS WITH SHREDDED COCONUT 16

BUTTERMILK TEA COOKIES WITH LEMON GLAZE & POPPY SEEDS 18

TOASTED ALMOND COCONUT MACAROONS 20

CHOCOLATE COCONUT MACAROONS 22

CLASSIC CHOCOLATE CHIP COOKIES 23

DECADENT CHOCOLATE COINS 24

RASPBERRY COCONUT OAT BARS 26

OLD-FASHIONED LEMON BARS 27

OLD-FASHIONED GRAHAM CRACKERS
with Turbinado Sugar

Graham crackers are the embodiment of nostalgia. I'd always been happy with the ones in the red box at the supermarket—until I tried our homemade ones. The difference in texture is immediately apparent. These cookies are less flaky and crumbly than the store-bought version, and they have a great snappy crunch. We also use a high-quality cinnamon, which has a nice spicy quality. (See photograph page 12.)

MAKES 24 COOKIES

2¼ cups all-purpose flour

¼ cup whole wheat flour

¼ teaspoon ground cinnamon

¼ teaspoon baking soda

¼ teaspoon table salt

½ cup (1 stick) unsalted butter, at room temperature

½ cup granulated sugar

¼ cup packed light brown sugar

¼ cup turbinado sugar (see Tip, page 36)

1. In a medium bowl, whisk together the flours, cinnamon, baking soda, and salt.

2. In the bowl of an electric mixer fitted with the paddle attachment, beat together the butter, granulated sugar, and brown sugar on medium speed until the mixture is light yellow and fluffy, about 3 minutes. With the mixer on low speed, add a third of the flour mixture and ¼ cup of water. Mix for 30 seconds. Repeat this step once, then add the remaining flour mixture and mix just to combine. Turn the dough out onto a lightly floured surface and knead by hand for about 10 seconds. Divide the dough in half. Cover one half with plastic wrap and set it aside.

3. Place a sheet of parchment paper on a work surface, put the dough on the parchment, and top with a second sheet of parchment. Roll the dough out to about ⅛-inch thickness. Repeat with the second half of the dough. Chill the dough for about 30 minutes.

4. Preheat the oven to 350°F.

5. Remove the dough from the refrigerator, peel off both sheets of parchment, and put the dough on a cutting board. Using a square cookie cutter, cut out the dough, rerolling the scraps twice. Put the cookies on a parchment paper–lined baking sheet. Sprinkle each cookie with a pinch of turbinado sugar.

6. Bake, rotating the sheet halfway through, for 20 minutes, or until the cookies are a dark golden color around the edges. Let cool for 10 minutes, then transfer to a wire rack to cool completely.

SPICED GINGER OATMEAL DROPS

I've always been a fan of strong, bold flavors. When I eat something, I want to taste it! In the early days of One Girl Cookies, when I was developing the Classic Collection, there was plenty of sweet but not enough spice. I fixed that problem by adding this cookie, which packs a gingery punch. I think there is an "Oh my!" moment when you bite into a little chunk of the candied ginger. It's an all-grown-up version of a childhood favorite, the oatmeal raisin cookie.

**MAKES ABOUT
30 COOKIES**

1½ cups all-purpose flour

1 tablespoon ground cinnamon

1 teaspoon ground ginger

½ teaspoon table salt

1 cup candied ginger, finely chopped

2½ cups old-fashioned rolled oats

1 cup (2 sticks) unsalted butter, at room temperature

1 cup packed light brown sugar

1 large egg

1 teaspoon vanilla extract

1. In a medium bowl, whisk together the flour, cinnamon, ground ginger, and salt. Stir in the candied ginger and the oats.

2. In the bowl of an electric mixer fitted with the paddle attachment, beat together the butter and brown sugar on medium speed until light yellow and fluffy, about 3 minutes. Scrape down the sides of the bowl. Add the egg and vanilla, and mix on medium speed for 1 minute. Reduce the speed to low, add the flour mixture, and mix for 30 seconds.

3. Take the mixing bowl off the mixer and finish mixing the dough with a rubber spatula, about 30 seconds. Cover the bowl with plastic wrap and refrigerate the dough for at least 1 hour, or overnight if possible.

4. Preheat the oven to 350°F.

5. Using a small cookie scoop or a spoon, scoop out a small round of dough, about 1½ tablespoons in size. Roll the scoop into a ball between the palms of your hands, and place it on a paper parchment–lined baking sheet. Gently press the ball onto the baking sheet. Repeat, leaving 1 inch between cookies.

6. Bake the cookies for 14 to 16 minutes, until they have darkened slightly. Transfer the cookies to a wire rack and let them cool.

VARIATION

There's nothing to be ashamed of if you are more of a traditionalist. Don't be shy—add ¾ cup of raisins or dried currants when you add the flour to the cookie dough.

ORANGE BUTTER DROPS
with Shredded Coconut

There's a secret here, and I'm about to share it. The beauty of this cookie lies in its texture—golden on the outside, almost creamy on the inside—and that texture comes from cream cheese. The kicker is that cream cheese has a tangy flavor, and when it is matched with the zestiness of the orange and the sweetness of the coconut, it makes for a definitively well-balanced sweet. It's called Sadie because a pretty cookie deserves a name to match.

**MAKES ABOUT
36 COOKIES**

¾ cup granulated sugar

Grated zest of 1 orange

2½ cups all-purpose flour

½ teaspoon table salt

1 cup (2 sticks) unsalted butter, cold, cut into pieces

1 teaspoon vanilla extract

3 tablespoons cream cheese, at room temperature

2 tablespoons fresh orange juice, or more if needed

1 cup confectioners' sugar, or more if needed

½ cup unsweetened shredded coconut (see Tip)

TIP: Both Bob's Red Mill (www.bobsredmill.com) and King Arthur Flour (www.kingarthurflour.com) sell great unsweetened coconut.

1. Put the granulated sugar and the orange zest in a medium bowl. Using both hands, rub the sugar into the orange zest. Put the mixture in the bowl of an electric mixer fitted with the paddle attachment, and add the flour and salt. Mix on low speed for 30 seconds.

2. With the mixer running on low speed, gradually add the pieces of butter. When the mixture begins to look like crumbs, add the vanilla. Gradually add 2 tablespoons of the cream cheese. When the dough starts to clump together, turn it out onto a lightly floured work surface. Knead it by hand for a few seconds until it is fully combined.

3. Preheat the oven to 350°F.

4. Scoop out a small round of dough, about 1½ tablespoons in size. Roll the scoop into a ball, place it on a parchment paper–lined baking sheet, and gently press the ball. Repeat, leaving 1 inch between cookies. Bake for 14 to 16 minutes, or until golden around the edges. Transfer to a wire rack to cool.

5. Prepare the glaze: In the clean bowl of an electric mixer fitted with the paddle attachment, combine the remaining 1 tablespoon cream cheese, the orange juice, and the confectioners' sugar. Mix on low speed for 30 seconds. Increase the speed to medium and mix for 2 more minutes. The glaze should be as thick as glue.

6. Spread the coconut on a plate. Dip the top of each cookie into the glaze, dip into the shredded coconut, and let set for 20 minutes.

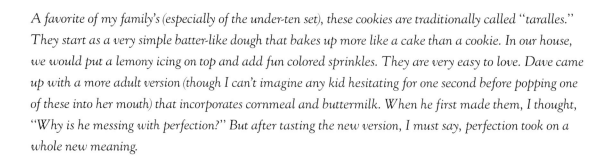

BUTTERMILK TEA COOKIES
with Lemon Glaze & Poppy Seeds

A favorite of my family's (especially of the under-ten set), these cookies are traditionally called "taralles." They start as a very simple batter-like dough that bakes up more like a cake than a cookie. In our house, we would put a lemony icing on top and add fun colored sprinkles. They are very easy to love. Dave came up with a more adult version (though I can't imagine any kid hesitating for one second before popping one of these into her mouth) that incorporates cornmeal and buttermilk. When he first made them, I thought, "Why is he messing with perfection?" But after tasting the new version, I must say, perfection took on a whole new meaning.

**MAKES ABOUT
24 COOKIES**

1½ cups all-purpose flour

¼ cup cornmeal

½ teaspoon grated lemon zest

¼ teaspoon baking soda

¼ teaspoon table salt

6 tablespoons (¾ stick) unsalted butter, at room temperature

¾ cup granulated sugar

1 large egg

½ teaspoon vanilla extract

⅓ cup buttermilk

Grated zest of 1 lemon

2 tablespoons fresh lemon juice

1¼ cups confectioners' sugar, or more if needed

¼ cup poppy seeds, for garnish

1. In a medium bowl, whisk together the flour, cornmeal, lemon zest, baking soda, and salt.

2. In the bowl of an electric mixer fitted with the paddle attachment, beat together the butter and sugar on medium speed until light yellow and fluffy, about 3 minutes. Scrape down the sides of the bowl. Add the egg and vanilla, and mix on medium speed for 1 minute. Reduce the speed to low, and mix in a third of the flour mixture and then half of the buttermilk. Scrape down the bowl. Add another third of the flour mixture and the remaining buttermilk.

3. Remove the bowl from the mixer, and fold in the remaining flour mixture with a rubber spatula until it is fully incorporated. Cover the bowl with plastic wrap and refrigerate for at least 1 hour, or overnight.

4. When you are ready to bake the cookies, prepare the lemon glaze: In a medium bowl, whisk together the lemon zest, lemon juice, and confectioners' sugar. The glaze should be as thick as glue. If the glaze is too thin, thicken it with additional confectioners' sugar. Set it aside.

5. Preheat the oven to 350°F.

6. Remove the dough from the refrigerator. Using a small cookie scoop or a spoon, place 1-tablespoon rounds of dough onto a parchment paper–lined baking sheet, leaving 1 inch between cookies.

7. Bake the cookies for 14 to 16 minutes, until they are golden around the edges. Let the cookies cool for 5 minutes on the baking sheet.

8. While the cookies are still warm, drizzle a small amount (about ½ teaspoon) of the lemon glaze over each cookie, and then sprinkle on ⅛ teaspoon of the poppy seeds.

9. Transfer the cookies to a wire rack to cool completely.

VARIATION

If poppy seeds aren't your thing, just forget about them and use some coarse sanding sugar instead.

TOASTED ALMOND COCONUT MACAROONS

One summer we were approached to do the wedding favors for an associate editor at Martha Stewart Weddings. Of course the answer was yes . . . to everything! The details of the order were very specific, and one request was that we do a coconut macaroon because it was the bride's favorite treat. It wasn't something we had done before, and we were committed to making ours just a little different and ten times better than those coconut globs found in cans. Dave added some toasted almonds, which resulted in a completely different incarnation of a standard coconut macaroon. We gave the cookie the name Sheila, after the blushing bride.

MAKES 36 MACAROONS

3 cups unsweetened shredded coconut (see Tip, page 16)

1 cup sliced almonds

⅛ teaspoon table salt

2/3 cup sweetened condensed milk

1 teaspoon vanilla extract

2 large egg whites

1. Preheat the oven to 350°F.

2. Spread the coconut out on a baking sheet, and toast it in the oven for 4 minutes. Transfer to a heatproof bowl and let it cool.

3. Put the almonds on the baking sheet and toast them for 8 minutes, then let cool. (Leave the oven on.) When they are cool enough to handle, put them in a food processor and pulse 3 or 4 times. Transfer to a large mixing bowl. Add the toasted coconut and the salt. Mix thoroughly.

4. In a medium bowl, combine the condensed milk, vanilla, and egg whites with a fork. Gently mix the egg white mixture into the coconut mixture until fully combined. Cover the bowl with plastic wrap and refrigerate for 20 minutes or so, for the flavors to develop.

5. Using a small cookie scoop or a spoon, scoop out small rounds of dough, about 1½ tablespoons each, onto a parchment paper–lined baking sheet, leaving 1 inch between cookies. Using your fingertips, form the dough into small dome-shaped cookies. If the batter is too sticky, wash your hands thoroughly and leave them a bit wet.

6. Bake the cookies for 12 to 14 minutes, until they have just the faintest golden color on their tips and sides. Do not overbake them or the cookies will be dry. Transfer the cookies to a wire rack to cool.

CHOCOLATE COCONUT MACAROONS

In my world, perfect pairs are Lucy & Ricky, Dolce & Gabbana, and chocolate & coconut. I'll take it in any form I can get it. And yes, I even mean a Mounds bar—I am not a snob when it comes to that combination. The weird thing is that I had been in business for over two years before we added a chocolate coconut cookie to the lineup. But it was worth the wait because Peggy is marvelously yummy. And it's even more special because we named it after Dave's favorite aunt, who has a huge role in many of the stories he tells me of his childhood. I never had the chance to meet her, but I'm certain that this fabulous cookie is a worthy memorial.

MAKES ABOUT 36 MACAROONS

1/2 cup semisweet chocolate chips

2 1/2 cups unsweetened shredded coconut (see Tip, page 16)

3/4 cup sugar

1/4 cup Dutch-processed cocoa powder

1/8 teaspoon table salt

2 large egg whites

1 teaspoon vanilla extract

1. Preheat the oven to 350°F.

2. Put the chocolate chips in a microwave-safe bowl, and heat on high power for 1 minute. Stir, and then heat for another minute until completely melted.

3. In a large bowl, combine the coconut, sugar, cocoa powder, and salt. Stir to combine.

4. In a small bowl, thoroughly mix the egg whites and vanilla with a fork. Stir the egg whites into the coconut mixture. Add the melted chocolate chips to the batter, and mix with a rubber spatula to combine.

5. Using a small cookie scoop or a spoon, scoop out small rounds of dough—about 1½ tablespoons each—onto a parchment-lined baking sheet, leaving 1 inch between cookies. Using your fingertips, shape each cookie into a neat little dome. If the batter is too sticky, wash your hands thoroughly and leave them a bit wet.

6. Bake the cookies for 12 minutes, or until they are slightly crisp on the outside but still soft inside. Do not overbake. Transfer the macaroons to a wire rack and let them cool completely.

CLASSIC CHOCOLATE CHIP COOKIES

I'll be the first to admit it: I swore One Girl Cookies would never make a chocolate chip cookie. Why bother? There were a million variations out in the world, many of them pretty tasty. My feeling was "Why reinvent the wheel?" Instead, I wanted to focus on interesting cookies that were more reminiscent of European treats. Well, our doors had not been open for more than a week before we had our first batch of Marys whipped up. The crowds (most of them under five years of age) demanded them. And so, we baked them. The moral of the story: Never say never. You just may end up eating your words (literally, in my case!).

Most people have a strong opinion about the style of their chocolate chip cookies. Crispy, chewy, or cakey? Semisweet, bittersweet, or milk? Big or small? Thin or thick? For us, it's all about cakey, bittersweet, small, and thick. Enough said.

**MAKES ABOUT
36 COOKIES**

2½ cups all-purpose flour

½ teaspoon baking soda

½ teaspoon table salt

1 cup (2 sticks) unsalted butter, at room temperature

1 cup packed light brown sugar

½ cup granulated sugar

2 large eggs

1½ teaspoons vanilla extract

3 cups semisweet chocolate chips

1. In a medium bowl, whisk together the flour, baking soda, and salt.

2. In the bowl of an electric mixer fitted with the paddle attachment, beat together the butter, brown sugar, and granulated sugar on medium speed until light yellow and fluffy, about 3 minutes. Add the eggs and vanilla, and mix on medium speed for 1 minute. Scrape down the sides of the bowl.

3. With the mixer on low speed, gradually add all of the flour mixture but stop mixing before it is completely incorporated. Add the chocolate chips and mix on low speed for 20 seconds. Cover the bowl with plastic wrap and refrigerate the dough for at least 1 hour, or overnight.

4. Preheat the oven to 350°F.

5. Remove the dough from the refrigerator. Using a small cookie scoop or a spoon, scoop out small rounds of dough, about 1½ tablespoons each, onto a parchment paper–lined baking sheet, leaving 1 inch between cookies.

6. Bake, rotating the sheet halfway through, for about 15 minutes, until the cookies are lightly browned. Transfer to a wire rack and let cool.

DECADENT CHOCOLATE COINS

I tend to be opposed to using the word "decadent" in the title of a dessert. I think it's sort of redundant, because isn't all dessert decadent? But this cookie goes above and beyond. It is really rich and chocolatey, but in an ever so subtle way—not that gooey and sugary sort of decadent, but much more refined and demure.

　　This cookie's name came about one Christmas season when we were trying to think of appropriate names for three holiday additions. We had three baristas at the time, so we decided to honor each of their grandmothers by naming a cookie after them. This one is Stephanie's grandma's namesake. (Jane, on page 33, is named after Rebecca's.)

(Jane, on page 33, is named after Rebecca's.)

**MAKES ABOUT
36 COOKIES**

1 cup semisweet chocolate chips

4 tablespoons (½ stick) unsalted butter, at room temperature

1 cup all-purpose flour

½ cup plus 2 tablespoons packed light brown sugar

2 tablespoons Dutch-processed cocoa powder

½ teaspoon table salt

2 large eggs

2 teaspoons grated orange zest

1. Put the chocolate chips and the butter into a microwave-safe bowl, and heat on high power for 1 minute. Stir them together, and then heat for 1 additional minute. You may need to heat the mixture for an additional minute or more, but be sure to stir the mixture thoroughly between heatings and do not overheat it. Let the chocolate cool for 5 minutes.

2. In a medium bowl, whisk together the flour, brown sugar, cocoa powder, and salt.

3. In the bowl of an electric mixer fitted with the paddle attachment, combine the eggs and orange zest and mix on low speed for 1 minute. With the mixer running on low speed, pour in the melted chocolate and mix for 1 minute, scraping down the sides of the bowl as needed. Add the flour mixture and mix on low speed for 10 seconds.

4. Turn the dough out onto a lightly floured work surface and knead it for about 30 seconds, until all of the flour has been incorporated and the dough comes together. Divide the dough in half; cover one half with plastic wrap and set it aside.

5. Place a sheet of parchment paper on a work surface, and put the other half of the dough on the parchment. Flatten the dough slightly with your hand and then top it with a second sheet of parchment. With a rolling pin, roll the dough out between the sheets of parchment to about ⅛-inch thickness. You can use a light dusting of flour if the

dough is sticky. Unwrap the other half of the dough and roll it out as you did the first half. Transfer the dough, still sandwiched between the parchment, to a baking sheet and chill it in the refrigerator for about 30 minutes.

6. Preheat the oven to 350°F.

7. Remove the dough from the refrigerator, peel off both sheets of parchment, and put the dough on a cutting board. Using a cookie cutter (you can use whatever shape you desire, but make it about 2½ inches in diameter), cut cookies out of the dough, rerolling the scraps once. Put the cookies on a parchment paper–lined baking sheet, spacing them 1 inch apart.

8. Bake the cookies for 10 to 12 minutes. The cookies are done when they begin to feel slightly firm and you can smell the chocolate. Be careful not to overbake them. Transfer the cookies to a wire rack and let them cool.

RASPBERRY COCONUT OAT BARS

Lots of people ask why it's important not to omit the bit of salt that most dessert recipes call for. It's a great question. Really, why bother when it's usually only a tiny amount? When you taste a cookie like Leona, which calls for a little more salt than usual, you'll understand why. That hint of salinity combined with the sweetness of raspberry jam . . . wow! Some would liken it to bottle rockets in your mouth.

MAKES 24 BARS

¾ cup unsweetened shredded coconut (see Tip, page 16)

1¼ cups all-purpose flour

¾ cup packed light brown sugar

⅓ cup granulated sugar

1 teaspoon table salt

12 tablespoons (1½ sticks) unsalted butter, cut into small pieces

1½ cups old-fashioned rolled oats

½ cup raspberry preserves

1. Preheat the oven to 350°F.

2. Spread the coconut out on a baking sheet and toast it in the oven for 2 to 3 minutes. Let cool. (Leave the oven on.)

3. Prepare a 9 × 13-inch baking pan by greasing it with cooking spray and then lining the bottom with parchment paper.

4. In the bowl of an electric mixer fitted with the paddle attachment, combine the flour, brown sugar, granulated sugar, and salt. Mix on low speed to combine. Add the butter and mix on low speed until the dough just starts to come together. Add the toasted coconut and the oats. Mix on low speed for 1 minute, until the dough has a crumbly texture.

5. Reserve ¾ cup of the dough. Transfer the remaining dough to the prepared pan. Using your fingers, press it evenly over the bottom of the baking pan. Bake, rotating the sheet halfway through, for 14 minutes, until the crust is golden around the edges. Let the crust cool for 10 minutes. Spread the raspberry preserves evenly over the crust, leaving a ½-inch border.

6. Crumble the reserved dough over the preserves. Bake for 7 minutes, or until the preserves are bubbling. Let the bars cool completely.

7. Loosen the edges of the crust with a small metal spatula. Invert the pan over a large baking sheet, releasing the bars onto the baking sheet. Remove the parchment paper, and invert the bars again onto a cutting board. Using a thin, sharp knife, cut them into 2-inch squares.

OLD-FASHIONED LEMON BARS

I need to confess that lemon bars never used to be one of those recipes I would regularly reach for. I found that sort of egg-yolky flavor unappealing. But since I always seemed to be in the minority on that matter, I knew we needed to offer them when we opened the shop. Our recipe has a more assertive lemon flavor with the same smooth texture people love. Prepare to pucker!

MAKES 24 BARS

CRUST

1 cup (2 sticks) unsalted butter, at room temperature

¾ cup granulated sugar

1 teaspoon vanilla extract

⅛ teaspoon table salt

2¼ cups all-purpose flour

FILLING

2 cups granulated sugar

Grated zest of 2 lemons

1 tablespoon all-purpose flour

4 large eggs

⅓ cup fresh lemon juice

Pinch of table salt

Confectioners' sugar, for dusting

1. Prepare a 9 × 13-inch baking pan by greasing it with cooking spray and then lining the bottom with parchment paper.

2. To make the crust, combine the butter and sugar in the bowl of an electric mixer fitted with the paddle attachment; beat on medium speed until the mixture is light yellow and fluffy, about 3 minutes. Add the vanilla and salt, and mix on medium speed for 1 minute.

3. Reduce the mixer speed to low, add the flour, and mix for 30 seconds. Put the dough on a lightly floured work surface, and knead it until it forms a smooth ball, about 30 seconds. Put it into the prepared pan, evenly press it over the bottom and ¾ inch up the sides, and prick the dough all over with the tines of a fork. Refrigerate for 20 minutes.

4. Preheat the oven to 350°F.

5. Bake the dough for 10 to 12 minutes, until the edge of the crust turns light brown. Let the crust cool while you prepare the filling.

6. To make the filling, working in a medium bowl, use both hands to rub the sugar into the zest. Add the flour and rub it into the mixture.

7. In a separate bowl, combine the eggs, lemon juice, and salt with a fork. Using a rubber spatula, gently fold the egg mixture into the flour mixture. Pour the filling into the baked crust. Bake, rotating the pan halfway through, for 30 minutes, until the top is golden along the edges and the center is set. Let cool completely.

8. Using a thin, sharp knife, cut the bars into 2-inch squares. Just before serving, dust them with confectioners' sugar.

Party Girl Cookies

lillian, aunt janet, aunt tina & mom, 1965, forest park, queens, ny

ESPRESSO CARAMEL SQUARES WITH WHITE & DARK CHOCOLATE SWIRL 30

CREAM CHEESE SHORTBREAD WITH TOASTED WALNUTS 33

APRICOT JAM–FILLED ALMOND BUTTER COOKIES 34

LEMON SHORTBREAD WITH FRESH ROSEMARY 36

WINTER SPICE COOKIE SANDWICHES WITH ORANGE CREAM 38

ALMOND SPIRALS 41

BITTERSWEET CHOCOLATE SANDWICHES FILLED WITH RASPBERRY PRESERVES 42

LEMON, OLIVE OIL, AND ALMOND BISCOTTI 44

DOUBLE CHOCOLATE & PISTACHIO BISCOTTI WITH CANDIED ORANGE ZEST 46

HONEY-NUT BARS ON AN ALMOND CRUST 48

ESPRESSO CARAMEL SQUARES
with White & Dark Chocolate Swirl

I've always called Lucia a gourmet Twix bar, because it bears a striking resemblance to that candy. With luscious caramel, a slight hint of espresso, and bittersweet chocolate, it's a crowd pleaser. But being popular does not come easy. It takes effort. In this case, that takes the form of lots of stirring of hot, bubbling caramel. Trust me when I say it is well worth it . . . and not just because I named it after my great-grandmother (see photograph page 28).

MAKES 24 SQUARES

CRUST
2 cups all-purpose flour

¼ cup sugar

Pinch of table salt

12 tablespoons (1½ sticks) cold unsalted butter, cut into pieces

CARAMEL
1 (14-ounce) can sweetened condensed milk

¼ cup sugar

1 tablespoon instant espresso or coffee granules

8 tablespoons (1 stick) unsalted butter

3 tablespoons light corn syrup

CHOCOLATE LAYER
1½ cups high-quality bittersweet chocolate chips

3 tablespoons white chocolate chips

1. Prepare a 9 × 13-inch baking pan by greasing it with cooking spray and then lining the bottom with parchment paper.

2. To make the crust, combine the flour, sugar, and salt in the bowl of an electric mixer fitted with the paddle attachment. With the machine running on low speed, gradually add the pieces of butter. Raise the speed to medium-low and mix for 3 minutes, until all of the butter has been incorporated.

3. Turn the dough out into the prepared pan, and evenly press it over the bottom. Prick the dough all over with the tines of a fork. Refrigerate the dough for 20 minutes.

4. Preheat the oven to 350°F.

5. Bake, rotating the pan halfway through, for 11 minutes, until it is golden around the edges. Let cool.

6. To make the caramel, combine the sweetened condensed milk, sugar, coffee granules, butter, and corn syrup in a medium heavy-bottomed saucepan set over low heat. Stir constantly until the butter begins to melt. Increase the temperature to medium-low, and continue to stir until the mixture begins to boil. Cook for 8 to 10 minutes, until the caramel is thick enough that when you drag the spoon through the middle, the indentation remains for 2 seconds. Be very careful at this point because the caramel is very hot.

TIP: After cutting these into squares, you'll be left with the not-so-attractive edges. We cut them into bits, freeze them, and then toss them on top of ice cream.

7. Pour the caramel over the crust and spread it out in an even layer, working quickly, as the caramel will firm up as it cools. Let the caramel cool completely.

8. Loosen the edges of the crust with a metal spatula. Invert the pan over a large baking sheet, releasing the bars onto the baking sheet. Remove the parchment, and invert the bars again onto a cutting board.

9. To make the chocolate layer, put the bittersweet chocolate in a microwave-safe bowl. Heat it on high power in 1-minute intervals, stirring between heatings to prevent the chocolate from burning, until it has melted. Spread the chocolate evenly over the caramel.

10. In a second microwave-safe bowl, melt the white chocolate in the same way. Using a pastry bag (or a plastic sandwich bag with a small hole cut into one corner), pipe stripes of white chocolate over the dark chocolate.

11. Let the chocolate layer cool for 20 minutes. When the chocolate is almost set but not quite hard, use a small, thin paring knife to cut 2-inch squares. The caramel can be messy, so be sure to clean the knife after each cut.

CREAM CHEESE SHORTBREAD
with Toasted Walnuts

Jane it is, plain it's not. Well, plainly delicious, yes, definitely. The crumb of this cookie is so fine and light that it literally melts in your mouth. For this reason, I have the ability to eat many of them. The other reason I am a big fan of Janes is that I'm a sucker for a flavorful but very simple cookie. It's undoubtedly something I get from my mom, who prefers sweets that are sans chocolate, buttercream, or any of the other things that attract many other people to a dessert. This cookie would be the one she would pick off of a gigantic platter of holiday treats. I probably would too.

MAKES ABOUT 36 COOKIES

1 cup walnuts

2 cups all-purpose flour

1 teaspoon table salt

12 tablespoons (1½ sticks) unsalted butter, at room temperature

4 ounces cream cheese, at room temperature

¾ cup sugar

1 teaspoon vanilla extract

TIP: If you can find dulce de leche at your market and you're in a sassy mood, go ahead and sandwich two of these cookies together with some of the caramel spread.

1. Preheat the oven to 350°F.

2. Place the walnuts on a baking sheet and toast them in the oven for about 10 minutes. Let the nuts cool (leave the oven on). When the walnuts are cool enough to handle, put them in a food processor and pulse 2 or 3 times, until all of the large pieces have been chopped.

3. In a medium bowl, whisk together the flour and salt. Add the chopped walnuts, and stir to combine.

4. In the bowl of an electric mixer fitted with the paddle attachment, beat together the butter, cream cheese, and sugar on medium speed until the mixture is light yellow and fluffy, about 3 minutes. Scrape down the sides of the bowl with a rubber spatula. Add the vanilla and mix on medium speed for 1 minute. Reduce the mixer speed to low, add the flour mixture, and mix for 20 seconds. Take the mixing bowl off the mixer and finish mixing the dough with a rubber spatula.

5. Scoop out a small round of dough, about 1½ tablespoons in size. Roll the scoop into a ball, place it on a parchment paper–lined baking sheet, and gently press the ball. Repeat, leaving 1 inch between cookies.

6. Bake the cookies for 14 to 16 minutes, until they are light brown around the edges. Transfer the cookies to a wire rack and let them cool.

APRICOT JAM-FILLED
ALMOND BUTTER COOKIES

Penelope

I am often asked which cookie is my favorite. I compare this query to picking a favorite child, but if pressed Penelope has a good shot at winning the contest. If I may say it out loud, our version of the thumbprint could very well be the best I've encountered. There, I said it. It's that buttery, nutty, fruity thing happening that is so appealing. Sort of the same way a warm piece of raisin toast slathered with butter and jam tastes so good. Buttery and fruity just hits the spot. Not to mention, when you open one of our gift boxes, Penelope screams, "Ain't I pretty?" The answer is, "You sure are."

**MAKES ABOUT
24 COOKIES**

1³⁄4 cups all-purpose flour

1⁄2 teaspoon plus a pinch of table salt

1 cup (2 sticks) unsalted butter, at room temperature

1⁄2 cup packed light brown sugar

2 large egg yolks

1 teaspoon vanilla extract

1⁄2 cup slivered almonds

2 tablespoons chopped walnuts

1 cup apricot jam

1 large egg white

1. In a medium bowl, whisk together the flour and the 1⁄2 teaspoon salt.

2. In the bowl of an electric mixer fitted with the paddle attachment, beat together the butter and the brown sugar on medium speed until the mixture is light yellow and fluffy, about 3 minutes. Add the egg yolks and vanilla, and mix on medium speed for 1 minute. Reduce the mixer speed to low and slowly add the flour mixture, stopping mixing before all of the flour is fully incorporated.

3. Remove the bowl from the mixer and finish mixing with a spatula until all of the ingredients are fully incorporated. Cover the bowl with plastic wrap and refrigerate the dough for at least 1 hour, or overnight if possible.

4. Preheat the oven to 350°F.

5. Put the almonds and walnuts on a baking sheet and toast them in the oven for 6 minutes, or until they are well browned and fragrant. Let them cool (leave the oven on). When the nuts are cool enough to handle, transfer them to a food processor and grind them to a fine powder. Transfer the powder to a medium bowl.

6. Put the apricot jam in the food processor and puree for 2 to 3 minutes, until it is very smooth.

TIP: Don't use too much egg wash on the cookies. The nuts clump together if the cookie is too wet.

7. Remove the dough from the refrigerator. Using a small cookie scoop or a spoon, form small rounds of dough—about 1½ tablespoons each—and put them on a parchment paper–lined baking sheet.

8. In a small bowl, combine the egg white, remaining pinch of salt, and 1 teaspoon of water. Beat with a fork until it is a bit frothy. Using a pastry brush, brush a small amount of the egg white mixture over the top of each cookie. Then dip the top of each cookie into the ground nuts. Return the cookies to the parchment-lined baking sheet, spacing them 1 inch apart. Let the cookies come to room temperature, about 10 minutes.

9. Using the tip of your ring finger (or your pinkie if you prefer), make an indentation in the middle of each cookie, pushing almost all the way to the bottom. (Although not exactly a thumbprint, it's close!)

10. Bake the cookies for 14 to 16 minutes, until they are golden around the edges. Remove the baking sheet from the oven. Using a pastry bag (or a plastic sandwich bag with a small hole cut into one corner), pipe the apricot puree into the "thumbprints" in the cookies. Return the baking sheet to the oven and bake for 4 minutes. Remove the cookies before the jam begins to boil. (This step helps the jam set.) Transfer the cookies to a wire rack to cool completely.

VARIATION

Penelope is beautifully versatile. Fill the imprint with whatever you've got a hankering for. Past versions that we've done include raspberry jam, fig jam, and orange marmalade.

LEMON SHORTBREAD
with Fresh Rosemary

Lena

This cookie is near and dear to me for a couple of reasons. First, it is named after my mom, who is responsible for teaching me all I know and love about food. Second, we created this cookie to give to guests at our wedding. We chose rosemary because it is often included in Italian wedding bouquets to signify fidelity—plus the bride (me!) loves herbs and spices in dessert. The rosemary flavor comes through at the end, almost after you are done enjoying the flaky cookie with the little sugar crunch on top. The lemon zest provides complexity and a nice complementary flavor. For our takeaway, we paired a few cookies with Jordan almonds, which Italians believe represent the wishes a couple makes on their wedding day.

MAKES 36 COOKIES

3 cups all-purpose flour

1 teaspoon table salt

1 cup (2 sticks) unsalted butter, at room temperature

3/4 cup granulated sugar

2 tablespoons grated lemon zest

2 tablespoons chopped fresh rosemary

1 large egg

1 teaspoon vanilla extract

Turbinado sugar (see Tip), for sprinkling

TIP: Turbinado, a type of sugar, can be found in most specialty food stores. Sugar in the Raw is a widely available brand.

1. Whisk the flour and salt together in a medium bowl.

2. In the bowl of an electric mixer fitted with the paddle attachment, beat together the butter and sugar on medium speed until the mixture is light yellow and fluffy, about 3 minutes. Add the lemon zest and rosemary, and mix for 30 seconds. Add the egg and vanilla, and mix for 1 minute. Reduce the mixer speed to low and gradually add the flour mixture. Mix until the dough just comes together. Do not overmix.

3. Turn the dough out onto a work surface. Dust with flour and divide in half. Place a sheet of parchment paper on a work surface, put half of the dough on the parchment, and top it with a second sheet of parchment. Roll the dough out to about ⅛-inch thickness. Repeat with the second half of the dough. Chill the dough for about 30 minutes.

4. Preheat the oven to 350°F.

5. Remove the dough from the refrigerator, peel off both sheets of parchment, and put the dough on a cutting board. Using a 3-inch round cookie cutter, cut out the dough, rerolling the scraps once. Place the cookies on a parchment-lined baking sheet. Sprinkle a pinch of Turbinado sugar on top of each cookie.

6. Bake the cookies for 10 to 12 minutes, until they are slightly golden around the edges. Transfer the cookies to a wire rack to cool completely.

WINTER SPICE
COOKIE SANDWICHES
with Orange Cream

Each December at the shop, we offer three new tea cookies that scream holiday. They are comprised of those flavors that urge you to belt out a rendition of "Frosty the Snowman." This pretty little thing started out as one of those "here for the season" cookies, but she seems to make her way back into the shop's case regularly. We think it's because there is something so classic, yet so modern, about this sandwich: two spice cookies that are sort of gingersnappy held together by an orange cream. Dave thought his great-aunt Florence would like it, so we named it after her.

MAKES 36 COOKIES

COOKIES

½ cup (1 stick) unsalted butter, at room temperature

¼ cup packed light brown sugar

¼ cup granulated sugar

2½ cups all-purpose flour

2 teaspoons ground ginger

½ teaspoon ground cinnamon

½ teaspoon baking soda

½ teaspoon table salt

FILLING

¼ cup cream cheese, at room temperature

2 tablespoons unsalted butter, at room temperature

Grated zest of 2 oranges

2 cups confectioners' sugar

1. To make the cookies, combine the butter, brown sugar, and granulated sugar in the bowl of an electric mixer fitted with the paddle attachment. Beat on medium speed until the mixture is light yellow and fluffy, about 3 minutes.

2. In a separate bowl, whisk together the flour, ginger, cinnamon, baking soda, and salt.

3. With the mixer running on low speed, add a third of the flour mixture and then ¼ cup of water. Mix for 30 seconds and then scrape down the sides of the bowl with a rubber spatula. Repeat this step one time. Add the remaining third of the flour mixture and mix until just combined. Some of the dry ingredients will not be fully mixed into the dough.

4. Turn the dough out onto a lightly floured work surface and knead it until all of the flour has been incorporated and the dough comes together, about 30 seconds. Divide the dough in half; cover one half with plastic wrap and set it aside.

5. Place a sheet of parchment paper on a work surface, and put the other half of the dough on the parchment. Flatten the dough slightly with your hand, and then top it with a second sheet of parchment. Using a rolling pin, roll the dough out between the sheets of parchment paper to about ⅛-inch thickness. You can use a light dusting of flour if the

TIP: You can be whimsical with the spices you use in this cookie. If you prefer a little nutmeg and less ginger, feel free to mix it up!

dough is sticky. Repeat with the second half of the dough. Transfer the dough, still sandwiched between parchment, to a baking sheet and chill it in the refrigerator for about 30 minutes.

6. Preheat the oven to 350°F.

7. Remove the dough from the refrigerator, peel off both sheets of parchment, and put the dough on a cutting board. Using a holiday cookie cutter (stars are my favorite), cut out the dough. Place the cookies on a parchment-lined baking sheet. Reserve the scraps of dough; they can be rerolled twice to make more cookies.

8. Bake the cookies for 8 minutes. Rotate the baking sheet and bake for 8 to 10 more minutes, until the cookies are a dark golden color around the edges. Let the cookies cool for about 10 minutes on the baking sheet, and then transfer them to a wire rack. Let the cookies cool completely.

9. To make the filling, combine the cream cheese and butter in the bowl of an electric mixer fitted with the paddle attachment. Beat on medium speed until the mixture is light yellow and fluffy, about 3 minutes. Add the orange zest and 1 cup of the confectioners' sugar. Mix for 1 minute on medium speed. Thoroughly scrape down the paddle and the mixing bowl, and then add the remaining 1 cup confectioners' sugar. Mix on low speed for 2 minutes. If the filling is too stiff, you can lighten it with a few drops of orange juice.

10. Turn half of the cookies over so they are bottom-side up. Using a pastry bag or a small butter knife, put a small dollop of the cream filling on each cookie bottom. Top the cream with the remaining cookies. Place the cookies on a clean baking sheet. They will need to rest at room temperature for a few minutes before the sandwiches are firm enough to handle.

ALMOND SPIRALS

Several years ago, a bride-to-be requested we provide her wedding favors. She had a magazine clipping of some knot cookies in a clear box, wrapped with ribbon. Without a recipe, we had some figuring-out to do. Using the photo she provided for inspiration, Dave created these pretty cookies. His version is more of a circle, representing the eternity of marriage (have I mentioned that he is a true romantic?). His flavor choices were symbolic as well: almonds, which for centuries have symbolized well wishes for the couple, and sugar, because marriage is so sweet!

MAKES ABOUT 24 KNOTS

¾ cup plus 1 tablespoon all-purpose flour

½ teaspoon table salt

½ cup (1 stick) unsalted butter, at room temperature

½ cup sugar

⅓ cup sliced blanched almonds, finely ground

1. In a medium bowl, whisk together the flour and salt.

2. In the bowl of an electric mixer fitted with the paddle attachment, beat together the butter and ¼ cup of the sugar on medium speed until the mixture is light yellow and fluffy, about 3 minutes. Scrape down the sides of the bowl with a rubber spatula. With the mixer running on low speed, add the flour mixture and beat for 10 seconds. Scrape the bowl again with the rubber spatula. Add the ground almonds and beat for 20 seconds.

3. Preheat the oven to 350°F.

4. Turn the dough out onto a lightly floured work surface. Knead the dough 2 or 3 times, adding a bit more flour if it is too sticky. With a small cookie scoop or a tablespoon, scoop out small rounds of dough and set them on the working surface. Using your hands, roll each piece of dough into a 2-inch-long snake shape. Carefully roll each snake into a spiral, like a snail shell with a small hole in the center.

5. Put the remaining ¼ cup sugar in a medium bowl. Roll each round of dough in the sugar and put them on a parchment paper–lined baking sheet, leaving 1 inch between cookies.

6. Bake for 6 minutes. Then rotate the pan and bake for 5 more minutes, or until the cookies are very slightly golden around the edges. Transfer the cookies to a wire rack to cool completely.

BITTERSWEET CHOCOLATE SANDWICHES
Filled with Raspberry Preserves

Bitter and sweet are the yin and yang of this cookie. The wafer contains a generous amount of cocoa (use the darkest type you can find), which gives it a slightly bitter tang. The preserves make up for it with fruity sweetness. The combination of these elements is fitting for a cookie named after my high school English teacher, Lana Hiller. She is one of those rare specimens of teacher who stays in touch with dozens of former students (I'm lucky enough to be one of them). She gets such a kick out of seeing who we all have become as adults—and rightly, feels a sense of accomplishment for it. In school, she was tougher than some of my other teachers. As an angst-ridden teenager, I'm not sure I appreciated the challenge. Now as an older, wiser adult, I realize that she was pushing me to do my best and always did it gently but firmly. I am pretty sure that had an effect on how many of her students turned out.

MAKES 48 SMALL TEA COOKIES

3 cups all-purpose flour

⅓ cup Dutch-processed cocoa powder

1 teaspoon baking soda

½ teaspoon table salt

1 cup (2 sticks) unsalted butter, at room temperature

1¼ cups granulated sugar

¾ cup packed light brown sugar

2 large eggs

2 teaspoons vanilla extract

Raspberry jam

1. In a medium bowl, whisk together the flour, cocoa powder, baking soda, and salt.

2. In the bowl of an electric mixer fitted with the paddle attachment, beat together the butter, granulated sugar, and brown sugar on medium speed until the mixture is light yellow and fluffy, about 3 minutes. Add the eggs and vanilla, and mix thoroughly on medium speed for 1 minute. Reduce the mixer speed to low and gradually add the flour mixture, stopping two times to scrape down the sides of the bowl. Mix until the dough is just barely coming together. Do not overmix.

3. Turn the dough out onto a lightly floured work surface, and knead it until all of the flour has been incorporated and the dough comes together, about 30 seconds. Divide the dough in half; cover one half with plastic wrap and set it aside.

4. Place a sheet of parchment paper on a work surface, and put the other half of the dough on the parchment. Flatten the dough slightly with your hand, and then top it with a second sheet of parchment. Roll the dough out between the sheets of parchment to about ¹⁄₁₆-inch

TIP: Look for the darkest cocoa powder that you can find for this recipe, as it will add a decadent chocolate element to your cookies. Many small specialty food shops will have a special variety, like Valrhona or Guittard. King Arthur Flour's website also has a few excellent choices (www.kingarthur flour.com).

thickness. You can use a light dusting of flour if the dough is sticky. Repeat with the second half of the dough. Transfer the dough, still sandwiched between parchment, to a baking sheet and chill it in the refrigerator for about 30 minutes.

5. Preheat the oven to 350°F.

6. Remove the dough from the refrigerator, peel off both sheets of parchment, and put the dough on a cutting board. Using a round 1¾-inch cookie cutter, cut out the dough. Place the cookies 1 inch apart on a parchment paper–lined baking sheet. Reserve the scraps of dough, and reroll them to make more cookies.

7. Bake the cookies for 10 minutes. It can be tricky to tell when chocolate cookies are finished, so have faith that they are done after 10 minutes. If the first batch does not become firm after it cools, bake the second batch for 12 minutes. Let the cookies cool on the baking sheet for about 10 minutes, and then transfer them to a wire rack and let them cool completely.

8. To fill the cookies, turn half of them over so that they are bottom-side up. Using a pastry bag (or a plastic sandwich bag with a small hole cut into one corner), pipe a small dollop of jam onto each cookie bottom. Top with the remaining cookies. Allow the cookies to rest for 1 hour or more for the jam to set up.

VARIATION

Lana looks pretty when she's all decked out in frosting. For special occasions or parties, mix up some mocha buttercream frosting (see page 87) and spread a thin layer on the top cookie.

LEMON, OLIVE OIL,
AND ALMOND BISCOTTI

Butter really never had a place in my home, but olive oil is in my blood. I am Sicilian, after all. Back in Castelvetrano—the small Sicilian city where my mom was born—my family has an olive grove. They haul their olives to the oleificio each season to make their own oil. It's better than any store-bought version, hands down. When we visit, before we pack our bags to leave, cousin Andrea packs up a jug for us to take home. It is a way of saying "Thanks for visiting!" This is a curious custom in Italy, the idea of the hosts giving the gifts of appreciation rather than receiving them. The way I see it, we really make out on the deal. That jug is precious cargo because it contains what we consider to be liquid gold. It is reserved for only the most special recipes, and this one certainly makes the cut.

MAKES 48 BISCOTTI

1 cup whole almonds, skins on

2 large eggs

Grated zest of 2 Meyer lemons (see Tips)

1 cup sugar

½ cup Sicilian olive oil (see Tips)

1 teaspoon vanilla extract

2½ cups all-purpose flour

1 teaspoon baking powder

½ teaspoon table salt

1. Preheat the oven to 350°F.

2. Put the almonds on a baking sheet and toast them in the oven for 15 minutes, or until they are well browned and fragrant. Let the nuts cool (leave the oven on). When the almonds are cool enough to handle, put them in a food processor and pulse 5 or 6 times, until ground.

3. In the bowl of an electric mixer fitted with the paddle attachment, combine the eggs, lemon zest, sugar, olive oil, and vanilla. Mix on medium speed for 1 minute.

4. In a medium bowl, whisk together the ground almonds, flour, baking powder, and salt. With the mixer running on low speed, gradually add the flour mixture to the egg mixture, stopping two or three times to scrape down the bowl. Mix until the dough is just beginning to come together. Do not overmix.

5. Scoop the dough out onto a parchment paper–lined baking sheet, and shape it into 2 equal logs. The dough should be sticky—you may need to wet your hands slightly with water in order to work with it. Each log should be about as wide as two knuckles on your middle finger and about ½-inch tall. Bake for 14 minutes. Rotate the baking sheet and

TIPS: If Meyer lemons are not available, you can substitute 2 regular lemons, or even the grated zest of 1 lemon and 1 orange.

The stronger the flavor of your olive oil, the more it will shine through in this recipe.

bake for 14 more minutes. Let the logs cool on the baking sheet for 12 to 15 minutes.

6. Reduce the oven temperature to 250°F.

7. Transfer the logs to a cutting board. Using a serrated knife, slice the logs into ½-inch-thick biscotti. Put the biscotti on the parchment-lined baking sheet, spacing them ½-inch apart. Bake for 7 minutes. Rotate the baking sheet and bake for 7 more minutes, or until the biscotti are slightly crisp on the exposed sides. Transfer them to a wire rack and let them cool completely.

VARIATION

I like it when citrus desserts have a little bit of salt. A modest sprinkle of fleur de sel on top of the biscotti before they go into the oven adds a delicious layer of flavor.

DOUBLE CHOCOLATE & PISTACHIO BISCOTTI
with Candied Orange Zest

In my early twenties, I made my first trip to Sicily with my childhood friend Karen. Part of our time was spent with the "strict" side of my family and the rest with the carefree, throw-caution-to the-wind side. My cousins Dino and Mariella headed up the wild-and-crazy team. Together, we visited all the sites, ate all the things, and smelled all the smells that I would most vividly remember about that trip. Gobbling piping hot chocolate cornetti (Italy's version of filled croissants) as we navigated hairpin turns at 75 miles per hour is something I will never forget. This cookie is my "mille grazie" to Mariella.

MAKES 48 BISCOTTI

CANDIED ORANGE ZEST
4 navel oranges

1 cup sugar

BISCOTTI
½ cup semisweet chocolate chips

¾ cup shelled pistachios, unsalted

2 cups all-purpose flour

½ cup Dutch-processed cocoa powder

1 teaspoon baking soda

¼ teaspoon table salt

6 tablespoons (¾ stick) unsalted butter, at room temperature

1 cup sugar

2 large eggs

1. To make the candied orange zest, use a citrus zester to cut long, thin strips of zest from the oranges. (You can use a vegetable peeler, but make sure you cut very thin strips of zest without much white pith). Put the zest in a small saucepan, cover with water, and bring to a boil over high heat. Then drain off the water. Repeat the boiling and draining process 2 more times. Set the drained zest aside.

2. In a clean saucepan, combine 1½ cups of water with the sugar, and bring to a boil. Stir in the orange zest. Simmer for 4 minutes, and then remove the pan from the heat. Let this mixture cool to room temperature before you handle it.

3. Preheat the oven to 350°F.

4. To make the biscotti, put the chocolate chips in a food processor and pulse 3 or 4 times to break them up. Add the pistachios and pulse 2 or 3 times.

5. In a medium bowl, whisk together the flour, cocoa powder, baking soda, and salt.

6. In the bowl of an electric mixer fitted with the paddle attachment, beat together the butter and sugar on medium speed until the mixture is

TIP: If you don't have the time to make your own candied zest, store-bought will work, or you can replace it with a couple teaspoons of freshly grated zest of orange.

light yellow and fluffy, about 3 minutes. Add the eggs and mix thoroughly on medium speed for 2 to 3 minutes.

7. Remove ¾ cup (loosely packed) of the candied orange zest from the syrup, allowing the excess syrup to drain back into the pan. Add the strained zest to the butter mixture, and mix on low speed for 30 seconds. Gradually add ¾ of the flour mixture, stopping two or three times to scrape down the bowl. Add the chocolate mixture and the remaining flour mixture. Mix until the dough is just barely coming together. Do not overmix.

8. Scoop the dough out onto a parchment paper–lined baking sheet, and shape it into 2 equal logs. The dough should be sticky—you may need to wet your hands slightly with water in order to work with it. Each log should be about as wide as two knuckles on your middle finger and about ½-inch tall.

9. Bake for 12 minutes. Then rotate the baking sheet and bake for 12 more minutes. Let the logs cool on the baking sheet for 12 to 15 minutes.

10. Reduce the oven temperature to 250°F. Transfer the logs to a cutting board. Using a serrated knife, slice the logs into ½-inch-thick biscotti. Put the biscotti on the parchment-lined baking sheet, spacing them ½-inch apart. Bake for 10 minutes, or until the biscotti are slightly crisp on the exposed sides. Transfer them to a wire rack and let them cool completely.

HONEY-NUT BARS
on an Almond Crust

Not long ago, I became mildly obsessed with honey. Well, it was more than just honey—it started with my interest in the whole colony collapse disorder and was fueled by my fascination with the role that bees play in our ecosystem. I even wanted to keep a hive, but at the time, bee-keeping was illegal in New York City. This bar cookie is a tribute to those hardworking critters that, until recently, have been very underappreciated. As far as the nuts go, I've always appreciated them, but they are particularly pretty in this recipe (especially the pistachios).

The earthiness of the nuts and the sweetness of the honey combine to achieve a near-perfect balance. The buttery crust ties it all together with a big bow.

MAKES 24 BARS

CRUST

1/2 cup whole almonds, skin on

2 1/2 cups all-purpose flour

1/2 cup sugar

1/4 teaspoon baking powder

1/2 teaspoon table salt

12 tablespoons (1 1/2 sticks) cold unsalted butter, cut into pieces

1 large egg

FILLING

3 cups whole unsalted nuts (any combination of almonds, hazelnuts, pistachios, and/or walnuts)

6 tablespoons (3/4 stick) unsalted butter

3/4 cup packed light brown sugar

1. Preheat the oven to 350°F. Prepare a 9 × 13-inch baking pan by greasing it with cooking spray and then lining the bottom with parchment paper.

2. To make the crust, put the almonds on a baking sheet and toast them in the oven for 20 minutes, or until they are browned and fragrant. Let them cool for 10 minutes (leave the oven on). When the almonds are cool enough to handle, put them in a food processor and pulse 8 to 10 times, until they are finely chopped. Add the flour, sugar, baking powder, and salt, and process for 1 minute to mix thoroughly. Add the butter and pulse 5 or 6 times, until it is the size of small peas.

3. In a separate bowl, lightly beat the egg. Add the egg to the processor and pulse until the dough just begins to form a ball.

4. Turn the dough out into the prepared pan, and using your fingers, press it over the bottom of the pan and 3/4 inch up the sides. Make sure the dough is fairly even in thickness. Prick the dough all over with the tines of a fork. Refrigerate the dough for 20 minutes.

5. Bake the crust for 10 to 12 minutes, until the edges turn light brown. Let the crust cool while you prepare the filling.

1/3 cup honey (see Tip)

1/4 teaspoon table salt

2 tablespoons heavy cream

TIP: Because there are precious few ingredients in the filling, each one really matters. I suggest using a high-quality honey for the best result.

6. Spread the nuts out on a baking sheet and toast them in the oven for 8 to 15 minutes, until they are browned and fragrant. (If using pistachios, do not toast them.) Let the nuts cool.

7. In a medium saucepan, combine the butter, brown sugar, honey, and salt. Stirring frequently, bring the mixture to a boil over medium-high heat. Add the cream and continue to stir until the mixture returns to a boil. Remove the pan from the heat. Be careful—the syrup will be very hot! Add all of the nuts to the syrup and stir to combine.

8. Pour the mixture over the crust, spreading it with a spatula. Bake for 15 to 20 minutes, until the center of the bars has begun to bubble. Remove the pan from the oven, and let the bars cool completely. Loosen the edges of the crust with a metal spatula. Invert the pan over a large baking sheet, releasing the bars onto the baking sheet. Remove the parchment paper, and invert the bars again onto a cutting board. Using a sharp knife, cut into 2-inch squares.

Cakes

nanny & poppy, 1936, orchard beach, bronx, new york

LEMON OLIVE OIL CAKE 52

CLASSIC ANGEL FOOD CAKE WITH PASSION FRUIT DRIZZLE 54

CHOCOLATE CHIP PISTACHIO POUND CAKE 57

PINEAPPLE UPSIDE-DOWN CAKE WITH HAWAIIAN SEA SALT 58

AUTUMN HARVEST CAKE 61

CHOCOLATE ZUCCHINI CAKE WITH CRÈME FRAÎCHE & BLACKBERRIES 62

MEYER LEMON LAYER CAKE WITH LEMON CURD,
LEMON BUTTERCREAM, & FLAKED COCONUT 63

SOUTHERN RED VELVET CAKE WITH CREAM CHEESE FROSTING 67

HUMMINGBIRD CAKE 68

BUTTERMILK CAKE WITH CHOCOLATE BUTTERCREAM & CANDIED ORANGE ZEST 70

RICH CHOCOLATE CAKE WITH SALTY DULCE DE LECHE
& HAZELNUT BRITTLE 73

LEMON OLIVE OIL CAKE

Lemons, olive oil, and sea salt embody Sicily, yet I am not sure that any of my relatives there have ever tasted a cake like this. It's so good that it's worth a trip back just to make it for them. I am pretty sure that it would quickly become part of the afternoon espresso ritual. The flavors are amazing, but it's the texture that is the real surprise. It is fine and light and reminiscent of an angel food cake, Italian-style.

**MAKES ONE
9-INCH CAKE**

1 cup cake flour

Grated zest of 1 lemon

5 large egg yolks

¾ cup granulated sugar

¾ cup olive oil

**1½ tablespoons fresh
lemon juice**

4 large egg whites

½ teaspoon table salt

**1 tablespoon turbinado
sugar (see Tip, page 36)**

1 teaspoon coarse sea salt

1. Preheat the oven to 350°F. Prepare a 9-inch round cake pan by greasing it with cooking spray and then lining the bottom with parchment paper.

2. In a large bowl, combine the cake flour and lemon zest. Using both hands, rub the zest into the flour, breaking up as many lumps of zest as possible.

3. In a large bowl, whisk together the egg yolks and ½ cup of the granulated sugar until the mixture has become light yellow, about 3 minutes. Add the olive oil and juice, and whisk for 1 more minute. Using a rubber spatula, fold in the flour mixture.

4. In the bowl of an electric mixer fitted with the whisk attachment, whip the egg whites until they are frothy, about 30 seconds. With the mixer running on medium-low speed, add the salt and the remaining ¼ cup granulated sugar. Increase the speed to high and whip until stiff peaks form. Using a spatula, carefully fold the whites into the batter. Make sure that all of the whites are incorporated. Pour the batter into the prepared pan, and sprinkle the turbinado sugar and the sea salt on the top.

5. Bake for 25 minutes. Rotate the pan and bake for 25 more minutes, or until a cake tester inserted in the center of the cake comes out clean. Remove the pan from the oven and let the cake cool in the pan for 20 minutes. The cake will shrink from the sides of the pan and have a rustic appearance. Turn the cake out onto a clean plate, remove the parchment paper, and turn the cake back over onto a wire rack. Let the cake cool completely.

CLASSIC ANGEL FOOD CAKE
with Passion Fruit Drizzle

This is one of those desserts that was born out of a "Eureka!" moment. We had been making angel food cakes for one of our wholesale clients, and one day we found ourselves with an extra one. Coincidentally (if you believe in coincidences), we had just filled a special order for passion fruit gelées for a wedding and had ended up with some extra fruit puree. Being the resourceful souls that we are, we created a glaze from the puree and poured it on top of the cake. It was nothing less than scrumptious and is now a staple at the shop. A word of warning, though: the aroma of the passion fruit curd cooking is amongst the headiest that I have ever encountered. You'll want it to stay in your kitchen forever, which may result in your making this cake a lot.

**MAKES 1 ANGEL
FOOD CAKE**

1 cup cake flour

1½ cups sugar

½ teaspoon table salt

**1½ cups egg whites
(from about 12 large eggs)**

**1 tablespoon plus
1 teaspoon fresh lemon
juice**

1 teaspoon cream of tartar

1 teaspoon vanilla extract

**¼ teaspoon almond
extract**

**Passion Fruit Drizzle
(recipe follows)**

1. Preheat the oven to 350°F.

2. Sift the cake flour, ¾ cup of the sugar, and the salt into a medium bowl three times. This is an important step, so don't cut corners!

3. In the bowl of an electric mixer fitted with the whisk attachment, combine the egg whites, lemon juice, cream of tartar, vanilla, almond extract, and 2 teaspoons of water. Beat on low speed for 30 seconds. Raise the speed to high and whip for 1 more minute, or until the egg whites are frothy. Slowly add the remaining ¾ cup sugar, and continue to beat until stiff peaks form, 2 to 3 minutes.

4. Using a rubber spatula, fold one-fourth of the sifted flour mixture into the beaten egg whites. Add another one-fourth of the flour and fold it in gently. Repeat until all of the dry ingredients have been carefully folded into the batter.

5. Carefully scoop (do not pour) the batter into an ungreased angel food cake pan with removable bottom. In a circular motion following the round shape of the pan, gently drag a thin knife through the batter to release any air bubbles.

TIPS: Look for passion fruit puree in the Latin foods section of your supermarket.

Note that this recipe requires an angel food cake pan. Do not butter or spray the pan and do not use a nonstick pan. The cake batter needs to "grip" the side of the pan in order to rise up. If you grease the pan, the cake will be dense and heavy.

6. Bake for 18 minutes. Gently rotate the pan and bake for 18 more minutes, or until the top is a rich golden brown and the cake springs back when pressed with your finger.

7. Remove the pan from the oven and turn it upside down. Let the cake cool completely while upside down.

8. To remove the cooled cake, run a sharp, thin knife around the edge of the cake and around the center tube. Carefully remove the cake from the outer part of the pan. Run the knife around the base of the cake. Carefully invert the cake onto a serving plate.

9. To serve, carefully drizzle the passion fruit glaze over the top of the cake.

PASSION FRUIT DRIZZLE

MAKES ½ CUP

1½ cups confectioners' sugar

3 tablespoons passion fruit puree (see Tips)

Combine the confectioners' sugar and the puree in a medium bowl, and whisk vigorously to combine. Just before using, warm the mixture in a microwave on high power for 30 seconds or in a saucepan over medium heat. This drizzle can be made up to 2 days ahead and kept in an airtight container in the refrigerator.

VARIATIONS

Take this cake up a notch by omitting the glaze. Instead, coat the cake in lightly sweetened whipped cream and then sprinkle a layer of big-flake coconut over the whipped cream. Move over, passion fruit! This cake is a knockout.

CHOCOLATE CHIP PISTACHIO POUND CAKE

Chocolate chip pound cake was a very popular after-school snack in my house when I was young. I distinctly remember breaking it into bite-size pieces in order to get the full effect of the warm, oozy chocolate chips. This recipe takes me back to those days, except that we've added pistachios for their beauty as well as their flavor. Needless to say, it's best when eaten warm, but try hard not to polish it off in one sitting.

MAKES ONE 9 X 5-INCH LOAF CAKE

1 cup semisweet chocolate chips

¾ cup shelled pistachios, unsalted

8 tablespoons (1 stick) unsalted butter, at room temperature

1 cup granulated sugar

3 large eggs

2 large egg yolks

½ teaspoon vanilla extract

1½ cups cake flour

½ teaspoon table salt

¼ teaspoon baking soda

¼ cup whole milk

2 teaspoons fresh lemon juice

1. Preheat the oven to 350°F. Prepare a 9 × 5-inch loaf pan by greasing it with cooking spray and dusting it with flour, knocking out any excess.

2. Put the chocolate chips in a food processor, and pulse 3 or 4 times to break them up. Add the pistachios and pulse 2 or 3 more times.

3. In the bowl of an electric mixer fitted with the paddle attachment, beat the butter and granulated sugar on medium speed until the mixture is light yellow and fluffy, about 3 minutes. With the mixer running on low, gradually add the eggs, egg yolks, and vanilla. Mix for 1 minute.

4. In a medium bowl, whisk together the cake flour, salt, and baking soda.

5. In a small bowl, mix together the milk and lemon juice. With the mixer running on low speed, mix in a third of the flour mixture and half of the milk mixture. Add another third of the flour mixture and all the remaining milk mixture. Remove the bowl from the mixer, and using a rubber spatula, fold in the remaining flour mixture and the chocolate-pistachio mixture. Spoon the batter into the prepared pan.

6. Bake, rotating the pan halfway through, for 45 minutes, or until a cake tester inserted in the center of the cake comes out clean. Let the cake cool in the pan for 20 minutes. Then turn it out onto a wire rack, and let cool completely.

PINEAPPLE UPSIDE-DOWN CAKE
with Hawaiian Sea Salt

When an intensely sweet fruit like pineapple meets heat, something magical happens. The sugars take on a whole new dimension and add rich complexity to the flavor. Herein lies the beauty of this cake. The salt here takes it to an intoxicating level. It may seem superfluous, but once it does a little hula dance in your mouth with the caramelized fruit, you'll realize it's not.

MAKES ONE 10-INCH
CAKE

12 tablespoons (1½ sticks) unsalted butter, at room temperature

1 cup packed light brown sugar

½ medium pineapple, peeled, cored, and cut into ½-inch pieces

1½ cups all-purpose flour

1½ teaspoons baking powder

½ teaspoon ground ginger

½ teaspoon ground cinnamon

½ teaspoon table salt

½ cup granulated sugar

2 large eggs

1 teaspoon vanilla extract

2 tablespoons dark rum

½ cup sour cream

1 teaspoon Hawaiian pink sea salt

TIP: Hawaiian sea salt is available in many specialty food stores. However, if you cannot find it, kosher salt is an acceptable alternative.

1. Preheat the oven to 350°F.

2. Melt 4 tablespoons of the butter in a 10-inch heavy-bottomed, oven-proof skillet set over medium heat. Add the brown sugar and stir to combine. Cook for 6 minutes. Then add the pineapple and cook for 1 more minute. Remove the skillet from the heat.

3. In a medium bowl, whisk together the flour, baking powder, ginger, cinnamon, and salt.

4. In the bowl of an electric mixer fitted with the paddle attachment, beat together the remaining 8 tablespoons butter and granulated sugar on medium speed until the mixture is light yellow and fluffy, about 3 minutes. With the mixer running on low speed, gradually add the eggs, vanilla, and rum. Mix for 1 minute.

5. With the mixer running on low speed, mix in a third of the flour mixture and half of the sour cream. Add another third of the flour mixture and the remaining sour cream. Remove the bowl from the mixer, and fold in the remaining flour mixture. Pour the batter over the pineapple in the skillet, and spread it out evenly.

6. Bake, rotating the skillet halfway through, for 50 minutes, or until a cake tester inserted in the center of the cake comes out clean. Let the cake cool in the skillet for 20 minutes. Run a sharp knife around the edges of the cake to loosen it from the skillet. Carefully invert the skillet over a serving plate, releasing the cake. Sprinkle the salt over the top of the cake.

AUTUMN HARVEST CAKE

Dave is committed to finding a place for local produce on our menu, even in the doldrums of a northeastern winter. This cake, an example of seasonality at its finest, highlights two New York State beauties, winter squash and apples. If, like me, you lament the passing of summer each year, this treat will help you get over it quickly and develop a new fondness for leaf raking and pumpkin carving.

MAKES ONE 9-INCH
CAKE

1 medium butternut
squash

1 teaspoon olive or
canola oil

2 cups all-purpose flour

1 teaspoon baking soda

1/2 teaspoon baking
powder

1 teaspoon table salt

1 teaspoon ground
cinnamon

1/8 teaspoon ground
cloves

1/8 teaspoon ground
nutmeg

8 tablespoons (1 stick)
unsalted butter, at room
temperature

1 cup packed light brown
sugar

2 tablespoons granulated
sugar

3 large eggs

1 teaspoon vanilla extract

1 crisp apple (such as
Braeburn, Empire, or
Crispin), peeled, cored,
and chopped

1 tablespoon turbinado
sugar (see Tip, page 36)

1. Preheat the oven to 350°F. Prepare a 9-inch round cake pan by greasing it with cooking spray and lining the bottom with parchment paper.

2. Cut the squash in half and scoop out the seeds and the strings. Rub the oil all over the cut surface of the squash, and place it, flesh side down, in a baking dish. Bake for 40 minutes, or until the squash is soft to the touch. Let the squash cool. When it is cool enough to handle, scrape the flesh from the skin. Measure out 1½ cups of the baked squash.

3. In a medium bowl, whisk together the flour, baking soda, baking powder, salt, cinnamon, cloves, and nutmeg.

4. In the bowl of an electric mixer fitted with the paddle attachment, beat together the butter, brown sugar, and granulated sugar on medium speed until the mixture is light yellow and fluffy, about 3 minutes. Add the eggs and vanilla, and mix on medium speed for 1 minute. Add the squash and the apples, and mix for 30 seconds. With the mixer running on low speed, add the flour mixture and mix for only 10 seconds. Take the bowl off the mixer and finish mixing the batter with a rubber spatula. Pour the batter into the prepared pan, and gently rap the pan on the countertop to even it out. Sprinkle the turbinado sugar over the top of the batter.

5. Bake, rotating the pan halfway through, for 50 minutes, or until a cake tester inserted in the center of the cake comes out clean. Let the cake cool in the pan for 20 minutes. Then turn the cake out onto a clean plate, remove the parchment paper, and then turn the cake back over onto a wire rack. Let cool completely.

CHOCOLATE ZUCCHINI CAKE
with Crème Fraîche & Blackberries

Each Labor Day weekend since Dave and I met, we have visited his family on Lake Canandaigua, in the Finger Lakes region of New York State. It is a beautiful place where the air is pure and the scenery pristine—a world away from Brooklyn. I always look forward to the annual trip and that we are guaranteed at least a couple of meals that make generous use of the vegetables from their backyard garden. The result of wonderfully fertile soil is that Dave's stepmom, Dee, is often called upon to use her gift of a green thumb to be creative in her uses of the garden's bounty. This cake is just such an example. In an effort to use one summer's overabundance of zucchini, she cleverly combined it with chocolate to create this extremely moist cake. It has a subtle vegetal flavor and interesting texture, only made better with a dollop of crème fraîche for just the right amount of sourness.

MAKES ONE
10-INCH CAKE

2½ cups all-purpose flour

½ cup Dutch-processed cocoa powder

2½ teaspoons baking powder

1½ teaspoons baking soda

1 teaspoon table salt

1 teaspoon ground cinnamon

2 cups sugar

¾ cup canola oil

3 large eggs

2 teaspoons vanilla extract

2 cups coarsely shredded zucchini

½ cup whole milk

1 cup crème fraîche

Fresh blackberries, for garnish

1. Preheat the oven to 350°F. Prepare a 10-inch round cake pan by greasing it with cooking spray and then lining the bottom with parchment paper.

2. In a medium bowl, whisk together the flour, cocoa powder, baking powder, baking soda, salt, and cinnamon.

3. In the bowl of an electric mixer fitted with the paddle attachment, beat together the sugar, oil, and eggs on medium speed until slightly frothy, 1 minute. Reduce the mixer speed to low, and add the vanilla and shredded zucchini. Mix for 30 seconds. Mix in a third of the flour mixture and ¼ cup of the milk. Scrape down the mixing bowl. Add another third of the flour mixture and the remaining ¼ cup milk. Remove the bowl from the mixer, and use a rubber spatula to fold in the remaining flour mixture. Pour the batter into the prepared cake pan. Lightly rap the pan on the countertop to release some of the air bubbles.

4. Bake, rotating the pan halfway through, for 50 to 55 minutes, until a cake tester inserted in the center of the cake comes out clean. Let cool in the pan for 20 minutes. Then remove the cake from the pan and let cool on a wire rack.

5. Serve each slice with a dollop of crème fraîche and the blackberries.

MEYER LEMON LAYER CAKE
with Lemon Curd, Lemon Buttercream & Flaked Coconut

Have I mentioned that if it were possible, I would consume coconut morning, noon, and night? I am pretty fond of lemon, too, so this cake is almost always the one I make for our family's celebrations. It's at its most fabulous when the buttercream is lightly colored (light green and pink are two of my favorites) so that there are bits of color peeking out from behind the coconut flakes. Plus, if you end up with a little extra lemon curd, you can make a delicious snack by spreading some on a bit of toast and adding some mascarpone, or you can mix it into some plain yogurt and if you're feeling really fancy, add some berries for your very own parfait.

MAKES ONE 9-INCH LAYER CAKE

1 cup (2 sticks) unsalted butter, at room temperature

2 cups sugar

5 large eggs

Grated zest of 2 Meyer lemons (see Tip, page 45)

2½ cups all-purpose flour

½ teaspoon table salt

½ teaspoon baking soda

1 cup sour cream

1½ teaspoons vanilla extract

Lemon Buttercream (recipe follows)

Lemon Curd (recipe follows)

1 cup dried coconut flakes (see Tip)

1. Preheat the oven to 350°F. Prepare two 9-inch round cake pans by greasing them with cooking spray and then lining the bottoms with parchment paper.

2. In the bowl of an electric mixer fitted with the paddle attachment, beat together the butter and sugar on medium speed until the mixture is light yellow and fluffy, about 3 minutes. Scrape down the sides of the bowl. Reduce the speed to low and add the eggs one at a time. Then add the lemon zest. Mix for 2 to 3 minutes, until fully combined.

3. In a large bowl, whisk together the flour, salt, and baking soda. In a separate bowl, mix the sour cream and the vanilla.

4. With the mixer running on low speed, mix in a third of the flour mixture and half of the sour cream mixture. Scrape down the bowl. Add another third of the flour mixture and all the remaining sour cream mixture. Remove the bowl from the mixer, and using a rubber spatula, fold in the remaining flour mixture until all of the ingredients are fully incorporated. Divide the batter between the prepared pans.

5. Bake for 15 minutes. Rotate the pans and bake for 15 more minutes, or until a cake tester inserted in the center of the cake comes out clean. Remove the cakes from the oven and let them cool in the pans for

(recipe continues)

TIP: For the best effect, it's important to use the big flaked coconut as opposed to shredded. If you prefer it toasted, don't hold back, though I think that the cake would look prettiest if the buttercream were left white.

20 minutes. Then turn each cake out onto a clean plate, remove the parchment paper, and then turn it back over onto a wire rack. Let the cakes cool completely.

6. To assemble, place a cake layer on a serving plate, and trim the top with a long serrated knife to make a level surface. Spread a thin layer of the lemon buttercream over the top. Using a pastry bag (or a plastic sandwich bag with a hole cut into one corner), pipe a ring of buttercream around the edge of the cake. This makes a sort of bowl for the lemon curd so that it will not spill out. Fill the bowl with 1 cup of the lemon curd. Place the second cake layer on top, being careful not to disturb the lemon curd. Spread the remaining buttercream over the entire cake. Press the coconut flakes into the buttercream on the sides of the cake.

LEMON BUTTERCREAM

MAKES 4 CUPS

8 tablespoons (1 stick) unsalted butter, at room temperature

6 cups confectioners' sugar

3 tablespoons whole milk, plus more if needed

1 teaspoon vanilla extract

1/2 teaspoon table salt

Grated zest of 2 Meyer lemons (see Tip, page 45)

In the bowl of an electric mixer fitted with the paddle attachment, beat the butter and confectioners' sugar on medium speed until the mixture is light yellow and fluffy, about 3 minutes. Scrape down the sides of the bowl. Reduce the mixer speed to low, and add the milk, vanilla, salt, and lemon zest. Scrape down the bowl and the paddle. Mix on low speed for 2 minutes, until the buttercream is thoroughly combined. If the buttercream is too stiff to spread, add an additional 1 to 2 teaspoons milk until you reach the desired consistency.

Extra buttercream can be stored in an airtight container, with plastic wrap pressed directly onto the surface of the buttercream, for up to 5 days in the refrigerator.

LEMON CURD

MAKES 1 CUP

4 large egg yolks

1/2 cup sugar

Grated zest of 1 lemon

1/4 cup plus 1 tablespoon fresh lemon juice

5 tablespoons unsalted butter, cut into pieces

Pinch of table salt

In a large metal bowl, whisk together the egg yolks, sugar, lemon zest, and lemon juice.

In a medium saucepan, bring about 2 inches of water to a boil. Place the metal bowl on top of the saucepan, and whisk the egg mixture constantly until the mixture coats the back of a spoon, about 5 minutes. Do not let the mixture come to a boil. Remove the bowl from the heat. Stir in the butter and salt until the butter melts completely.

Strain the curd through a fine-mesh strainer into a heat-resistant bowl. Press plastic wrap directly onto the surface of the curd to prevent a skin from forming. Chill the curd in the refrigerator for about 1 hour, or until it has set. The curd can be kept in the refrigerator, with plastic wrap pressed onto the surface, for about 5 days.

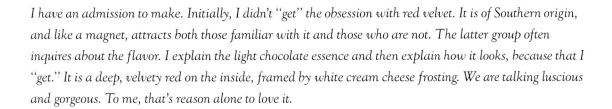

SOUTHERN RED VELVET CAKE
with Cream Cheese Frosting

I have an admission to make. Initially, I didn't "get" the obsession with red velvet. It is of Southern origin, and like a magnet, attracts both those familiar with it and those who are not. The latter group often inquires about the flavor. I explain the light chocolate essence and then explain how it looks, because that I "get." It is a deep, velvety red on the inside, framed by white cream cheese frosting. We are talking luscious and gorgeous. To me, that's reason alone to love it.

MAKES ONE 9-INCH
LAYER CAKE

2 cups plain whole-milk
yogurt

2 teaspoons vanilla extract

2 teaspoons red food
coloring

2 teaspoons distilled
white vinegar

16 tablespoons (2 sticks)
unsalted butter, at room
temperature

3 cups sugar

4 large eggs

4 cups cake flour

2/3 cup Dutch-processed
cocoa powder

2 teaspoons baking
powder

1 teaspoon baking soda

1 teaspoon table salt

Cream Cheese Frosting
(page 69)

1. Preheat the oven to 350°F. Prepare two 9-inch round cake pans by greasing them with cooking spray and then lining the bottoms with parchment paper.

2. In a medium bowl, combine the yogurt, vanilla, food coloring, and vinegar. Stir well.

3. In the bowl of an electric mixer fitted with the paddle attachment, beat together the butter and sugar on medium speed until light yellow and fluffy, about 3 minutes. Add the eggs one at a time and mix for 1 minute.

4. In a separate bowl, whisk together the flour, cocoa powder, baking powder, baking soda, and salt. With the mixer running on low speed, mix in a third of the flour mixture and half of the yogurt mixture. Add another third of the flour mixture and all the remaining yogurt mixture. Remove the bowl from the mixer, and fold in the remaining flour mixture until fully incorporated. Pour the batter into the prepared pans.

5. Bake, rotating the pans halfway through, for 40 minutes, or until a cake tester inserted in the center of the cake comes out clean. Let the cakes cool in the pans for 20 minutes. Then turn each cake out onto a clean plate, remove the parchment paper, and then turn it back over onto a wire rack. Let cool completely.

6. To assemble, place a cake layer on a serving plate. Spread a thin layer of the cream cheese frosting over the top. Place the second layer on top, and spread the remaining frosting over the entire cake.

HUMMINGBIRD CAKE

The name says it all. How can you not love a cake with such a sweet moniker? It just so happens that it tastes pretty divine as well. It is actually a Southern creation, and one thing is for sure: Southerners know their desserts. This layer cake is no exception. The banana-pineapple-pecan trio makes for a cake that is delightfully moist and slightly fruity. It's a fairly rich cake, so you'll want to cut thin slices—though guests will undoubtedly ask for seconds (see photograph on page 50).

MAKES ONE 9-INCH
LAYER CAKE

**1 pound ripe bananas
(5 or 6)**

**½ teaspoon fresh lemon
juice**

1½ cups chopped pecans

1 cup canola oil

2 large eggs

2 teaspoons vanilla extract

**1 cup canned pineapple
chunks, drained**

3 cups all-purpose flour

2 cups sugar

1 teaspoon baking soda

**½ teaspoon ground
cinnamon**

½ teaspoon table salt

**Cream Cheese Frosting
(recipe follows)**

1. Preheat the oven to 350°F. Prepare two 9-inch round cake pans by greasing them with cooking spray and then lining the bottoms with parchment paper.

2. In a food processor, combine the bananas and lemon and process until pureed.

3. Put the pecans on a baking sheet and toast them in the oven for 10 minutes, until they are browned and fragrant. Let the nuts cool for 10 minutes.

4. In the bowl of an electric mixer fitted with the paddle attachment, combine the oil, eggs, and vanilla. Mix on medium speed for 1 minute, until the ingredients are thoroughly combined. Add the banana puree and the pineapple chunks, and mix for 10 seconds. Scrape down the sides of the bowl.

5. In a large bowl, whisk together the flour, sugar, baking soda, cinnamon, and salt.

6. With the mixer running on low speed, add half of the flour mixture and mix for 10 seconds. Briefly scrape down the mixing bowl and paddle. With the mixer on low speed, add the remaining half of the flour mixture and 1 cup of the pecans. Mix for 10 seconds. Scrape down the bowl and paddle. Divide the batter between the prepared pans.

7. Bake for 17 minutes. Rotate the pans and bake for 17 more minutes, or until a cake tester inserted in the center of the cake comes out clean.

Remove the cakes from the oven and let them cool in the pans for 20 minutes. Then turn each cake out onto a clean plate, remove the parchment paper, and then turn it back over onto a wire rack. Let the cakes cool completely.

8. To assemble, place a cake layer on a serving plate. Trim the top of the layer with a long serrated knife to make a level surface. Spread a thin layer of the cream cheese frosting over the top. Place the second layer on top of the frosting, and spread the remaining cream cheese frosting over the entire cake. Sprinkle the remaining ½ cup pecans around the top edge of the cake.

CREAM CHEESE FROSTING

MAKES 4 CUPS

1 8-ounce package cream cheese, at room temperature

8 tablespoons (1 stick) unsalted butter, at room temperature

¼ teaspoon table salt

2 teaspoons vanilla extract

4½ cups (1 pound) confectioners' sugar, plus more if needed

In the bowl of an electric mixer fitted with the paddle attachment, beat together the cream cheese and butter on medium speed until soft and creamy, 5 minutes. Add the salt and vanilla, and mix for 30 seconds on low speed. Scrape down the sides of the bowl.

With the mixer running on low speed, add the confectioners' sugar. Scrape down the bowl, and then beat the mixture for 1 more minute. If the consistency is too soft for frosting the cake, add more confectioners' sugar, a tablespoon at a time, until you reach the desired consistency.

BUTTERMILK CAKE
with Chocolate Buttercream & Candied Orange Zest

Like other fine things in life, this cake takes time. It is the ideal recipe to break out on a rainy day when you feel like nesting. Needless to say, it is delicious, regardless of the weather, and so darn pretty and festive that it is worth any extra time it may require. It screams "Happy birthday!" or "Congratulations!" at the top of its lungs . . . and means it.

Here we suggest making your own candied orange zest, which you should start two hours ahead of time. It is fairly easy, but substituting store-bought will not cost you any points in our book. The buttermilk in the cake batter provides a sweet tang and the orange adds that citrusy goodness.

MAKES ONE 9-INCH LAYER CAKE

CANDIED ORANGE ZEST
2 navel oranges

¼ cup sugar

CAKE
2½ cups all-purpose flour

1 teaspoon table salt

½ teaspoon baking soda

1 cup (2 sticks) unsalted butter, at room temperature

2 cups sugar

4 large eggs

Grated zest of 1 orange

1 cup buttermilk

1½ teaspoons vanilla extract

1. To make the candied zest, remove long, narrow strips of zest from the oranges with a vegetable peeler. If there is any pith attached to the zest, remove it with a pairing knife. Place the zest in a small saucepan, cover with water, and bring to a boil over high heat. Then drain off the water. Repeat the boiling and draining process 2 more times. Set the drained zest aside.

2. In a clean saucepan, combine 1 cup of water with the sugar, and bring to a boil. Stir in the orange zest. Simmer for 4 minutes, and then remove from the heat. Let this mixture cool before you handle it.

3. To make the cake, preheat the oven to 350°F. Prepare two 9-inch cake pans by greasing them with cooking spray and then lining the bottoms with parchment paper.

4. In a large bowl, whisk together the flour, salt, and baking soda.

5. In the bowl of an electric mixer fitted with the paddle attachment, beat together the butter and sugar on medium speed until the mixture is light yellow and fluffy, about 3 minutes. Scrape down the sides of the bowl with a rubber spatula. With the mixer running on low speed, add the eggs one at a time, followed by the orange zest. Mix for about 2 minutes, until fully combined. Scrape down the bowl again.

(recipe continues)

CHOCOLATE BUTTERCREAM

¾ cup (three-fourths of an 8-ounce package) cream cheese, at room temperature

8 tablespoons (1 stick) unsalted butter, at room temperature

1½ teaspoons vanilla extract

½ cup Dutch-processed cocoa powder

4 cups confectioners' sugar, plus more if needed

6. In a separate bowl, mix together the buttermilk and vanilla. With the mixer running on low speed, mix in a third of the flour mixture and half of the buttermilk mixture. Scrape down the mixing bowl. Add another third of the flour mixture and all the remaining buttermilk mixture. Remove the bowl from the mixer, and using a rubber spatula, fold in the remaining flour mixture until all of the ingredients are fully incorporated. Divide the batter between the prepared cake pans.

7. Bake, rotating the pans halfway through, for 34 minutes, or until a cake tester inserted in the center of the cakes comes out clean. Let the cakes cool in the pans for 20 minutes. Then turn each cake out onto a clean plate, remove the parchment paper, and then turn it back over onto a wire rack. Let the cakes cool completely.

8. To make the buttercream, combine the cream cheese and butter in the bowl of an electric mixer fitted with the paddle attachment. Beat for about 4 minutes, until soft and creamy. Scrape down the sides of the bowl with a rubber spatula. Add the vanilla and mix for 30 seconds on low speed. Scrape down the bowl again.

9. With the mixer running on low speed, add the cocoa powder and the confectioners' sugar. Scrape down the bowl and continue to beat for 1 minute. If the consistency is too soft to use for frosting the cake, add more confectioners' sugar, a tablespoon at a time, until you reach the desired consistency. If it is too stiff, mix in a few drops of regular milk. The buttercream should be smooth and creamy and easy to spread.

10. To assemble, place a cake layer on a serving plate. Trim the top of the layer with a long serrated knife to make a level surface. Spread a thin layer of chocolate buttercream over the top. Chop 2 tablespoons of the candied orange zest and sprinkle it over the buttercream. Place the second layer on top of the frosting, and finish spreading the buttercream over the entire cake. Artfully arrange the remaining candied orange zest around the top edge of the cake.

RICH CHOCOLATE CAKE
with Salty Dulce de Leche & Hazelnut Brittle

I can imagine Argentinians chuckling when they hear about the recent dulce de leche craze in the States. After all, they have been enjoying this sweet, milky caramel for nearly two hundred years. Relatively new here, and often available in the specialty foods section of the supermarket, dulce de leche can be used in all sorts of ways, but we like to drizzle it on top of what could be considered the moistest, most delicious cake on the planet (I double-dare you to find a better one). The combination has a perfect salty-sweet thing happening that is like a highly addictive sensory overload. I promise, it will have you coming back for more. If it doesn't, perhaps the crumbled brittle that decorates the top will.

MAKES ONE
10-INCH CAKE

CAKE
1 cup freshly brewed hot coffee

1/2 cup Dutch-processed cocoa powder

3/4 cup packed light brown sugar

1/2 cup plain whole-milk yogurt

2 teaspoons vanilla extract

8 tablespoons (1 stick) unsalted butter, at room temperature

1 1/4 cups granulated sugar

2 eggs

1 1/4 cups all-purpose flour

3/4 teaspoon baking soda

1 teaspoon table salt

TOPPING
Hazelnut Brittle (recipe follows)

1/2 cup dulce de leche

1 1/2 teaspoons kosher salt

1. Preheat the oven to 350°F. Prepare a 10-inch round cake pan by greasing it with cooking spray and then lining the bottom with parchment paper.

2. To make the cake, pour the hot coffee into a medium bowl and stir in the cocoa powder until it dissolves. Stir in the brown sugar, followed by the yogurt and the vanilla. Stir thoroughly to ensure that all of the ingredients are incorporated.

3. In the bowl of an electric mixer fitted with the paddle attachment, beat the butter and granulated sugar on medium speed until light-yellow and fluffy, about 3 minutes. Scrape down the sides of the bowl. Add the eggs and mix for 2 minutes, scraping down the bowl as needed.

4. In a medium bowl, whisk together the flour, baking soda, and salt. With the mixer running on low speed, mix in a third of the flour mixture and half of the coffee mixture. Scrape down the bowl. Add another third of the flour mixture and all the remaining coffee mixture. Remove the bowl from the mixer and, using a rubber spatula, fold in the remaining flour mixture until all of the ingredients are fully incorporated. Pour the batter into the prepared cake pan.

(recipe continues)

5. Bake for 25 minutes. Rotate the pan in the oven and bake for 20 more minutes, or until a cake tester inserted in the center of the cake comes out clean. Remove the pan from the oven and let the cake cool in the pan for 20 minutes. Then turn the cake out onto a clean plate, remove the parchment, and turn the cake back over onto a wire rack. Let the cake cool completely.

6. In a food processor, pulse the brittle pieces 3 to 4 times until the brittle is powdery.

7. Put the cooled cake on a serving dish. In a microwave-safe dish, heat the dulce de leche on high power for 30 seconds, or until it is just liquid. Spoon the dulce de leche over the cake, and then sprinkle the kosher salt over the dulce de leche. Sprinkle about ½ cup of the ground brittle around the outer edge of the cake as a delicious decoration.

HAZELNUT BRITTLE

MAKES ABOUT 2 CUPS

½ cup whole unsalted hazelnuts, skins removed

6 tablespoons (¾ stick) unsalted butter

½ cup sugar

1 tablespoon light corn syrup

⅛ teaspoon baking soda

⅛ teaspoon table salt

Preheat the oven to 350°F.

Put the hazelnuts on a baking sheet and toast them in the oven for 15 minutes until browned and fragrant. Let cool.

Prepare a large baking sheet by lining it with parchment paper. Melt the butter in a heavy-bottomed saucepan set over medium heat. Whisk in the sugar and corn syrup, and bring to a boil. Continue whisking constantly until the syrup is a rich amber color, about 10 minutes. Remove the pan from the heat and carefully whisk in the baking soda and salt. Stir in the hazelnuts and then pour the contents of the pan onto the prepared baking sheet and spread it out into a thin layer. Let the brittle cool completely.

Break the brittle into 2-inch pieces. The brittle will keep in an airtight container for up to 1 week.

VARIATION

For a change of pace, replace the dulce de leche with mocha buttercream (page 87).

Whoopie Pies & Cupcakes

dad, 1944, bronx, new york

PUMPKIN WHOOPIE PIES WITH MAPLE SPICE FILLING 78

BANANA WHOOPIE PIES WITH DULCE DE LECHE FILLING 80

CHOCOLATE WHOOPIE PIES WITH PEPPERMINT FILLING 83

THE BEST VANILLA CUPCAKES WITH MOCHA BUTTERCREAM 85

THE BEST CHOCOLATE CUPCAKES WITH VANILLA BUTTERCREAM 88

CARROT CUPCAKES WITH CREAM CHEESE FROSTING 90

PUMPKIN WHOOPIE PIES
with Maple Spice Filling

Several years back, our friends Luke and Leslie invited us to their wedding. It took place in Lancaster, Pennsylvania, which happens to be the home of many things, including whoopie pies (people from Maine may argue this point, as there is an age-old feud over where they really were created). There were many memorable things about the wedding, but being the self-professed foodie that I am, what stuck in my mind was the whoopie pies in our hotel welcome baskets. Their version was made with a marshmallowy, shortening-based filling, but we saw great potential and couldn't wait to get back to our kitchen in Brooklyn and start tinkering.

That potential exploded almost instantly. Dave first introduced this whoopie pie as a café special. The intention was never to keep it as a regular item, but our customers had a different plan. Here we are, four years later, and you'll find them on our counter every day (see photograph page 76).

MAKES 24
WHOOPIE PIES

3 cups all-purpose flour

2 teaspoons ground ginger

1 teaspoon ground cinnamon

1 teaspoon baking powder

1 teaspoon baking soda

1 teaspoon table salt

1 (15-ounce) can pumpkin puree

2 cups packed light brown sugar

1 cup canola oil

2 large eggs

2 tablespoons dark molasses

Maple Spice Filling (recipe follows)

1. Preheat the oven to 350°F. Line a baking sheet with parchment paper.

2. In a medium bowl, whisk together the flour, ginger, cinnamon, baking powder, baking soda, and salt.

3. In the bowl of an electric mixer fitted with the paddle attachment, beat together the pumpkin puree, brown sugar, oil, eggs, and molasses for 3 minutes on medium speed. Thoroughly scrape down the bowl with a rubber spatula. With the mixer running on low speed, gradually add the flour mixture for a total mixing time of 30 seconds. Carefully scrape down the bowl again.

4. Using a pastry bag fitted with a large plain tip (the hole should be about as large as the tip of your ring finger), pipe 2-inch-diameter circles onto the prepared baking sheet, leaving 1½ inches between them. Be careful to keep your pastry bag completely vertical to achieve nice circles. (If you have to wait between batches of whoopie pies, keep the batter refrigerated.)

5. Bake for 10 minutes. Rotate the baking sheet and bake for 8 to 10 more minutes, until the whoopie pies are a deep orange color and spring back when touched. Let the whoopie pies cool completely.

6. To fill the whoopies, turn half of them over so that they are bottom-side up. Using a pastry bag, pipe a small dollop of the maple spice filling onto each whoopie bottom. Top with the remaining whoopies.

MAPLE SPICE FILLING

MAKES 2 CUPS

4 ounces cream cheese, at room temperature

5 tablespoons unsalted butter, at room temperature

1 tablespoon Grade B dark maple syrup

⅛ teaspoon ground cinnamon

Pinch of ground cloves

⅛ teaspoon table salt

3 cups confectioners' sugar, plus more if needed

In the bowl of an electric mixer fitted with the paddle attachment, beat together the cream cheese and butter on medium speed until the mixture is light and fluffy, about 3 minutes. Scrape down the sides of the bowl with a rubber spatula. Add the maple syrup, cinnamon, cloves, and salt, and mix for 30 seconds on low speed.

With the mixer running on low speed, gradually add the confectioners' sugar, and then beat for 1 minute. Scrape down the bowl. If the filling is too soft to hold its shape, add more confectioners' sugar, a tablespoon at a time, until you reach the desired consistency.

Store in the refrigerator, in an airtight container with plastic wrap pressed onto the surface of the filling, for up to 5 days.

BANANA WHOOPIE PIES
with Dulce de Leche Filling

We tend to take a somewhat purist stance when it comes to whoopies, usually filling them with vanilla cream—it's a tasty complement to whatever it is paired with. However, this caramel-banana combo was introduced to us recently (actually by a bride and groom who requested it as their wedding cake), and we decided to step out of our comfort zone and give it a whoopie whirl. The result is a lot of fun and a yummy change of pace.

MAKES 24 WHOOPIE PIES

1 pound ripe bananas

1/2 teaspoon fresh lemon juice

4 cups all-purpose flour

1 1/2 teaspoons baking powder

1/2 teaspoon baking soda

1 1/2 teaspoons table salt

1 cup canola oil

3 large eggs

1 cup granulated sugar

1 cup packed light brown sugar

1 teaspoon vanilla extract

Dulce de Leche Filling (recipe follows)

1. Combine the bananas and lemon juice in a food processor, and process until pureed.

2. In a medium bowl, whisk together the flour, baking powder, baking soda, and salt.

3. In the bowl of an electric mixer fitted with the paddle attachment, beat together the oil, eggs, granulated sugar, brown sugar, and vanilla on medium speed for 2 minutes. Scrape down the sides of the bowl with a rubber spatula. Add the banana puree and mix on low speed for 30 seconds. Scrape down the bowl again. With the mixer running on low speed, gradually add the flour mixture for a total mixing time of 30 seconds. Carefully scrape down the bowl. Refrigerate the batter for 30 minutes.

4. Preheat the oven to 350°F. Line a baking sheet with parchment paper.

5. Using a pastry bag fitted with a large plain tip (the hole should be about as large as the tip of your ring finger), pipe 2-inch-diameter circles onto the prepared baking sheet, leaving 1½ inches between them. Be careful to keep your pastry bag completely vertical to achieve nice circles. (If you have to wait between batches of whoopie pies, keep the batter refrigerated.)

6. Immediately put the baking sheet in the oven. Bake for 10 minutes without rotating the baking sheet. The whoopie pies are done when

(recipe continues)

they are slightly golden in color and spring back when touched. Let the whoopie pies cool completely.

7. To fill the whoopies, turn half of them over so that they are bottom-side up. Using a pastry bag, pipe a small dollop of the dulce de leche filling onto each whoopie bottom. Top with the remaining whoopies.

DULCE DE LECHE FILLING

MAKES 2 CUPS

4 ounces package cream cheese, at room temperature

5 tablespoons unsalted butter, at room temperature

1 teaspoon vanilla extract

¼ teaspoon salt

⅓ cup dulce de leche (available in the specialty section of the supermarket)

3 cups confectioners' sugar, plus more if needed

In the bowl of an electric mixer fitted with the paddle attachment, beat together the cream cheese and butter on medium speed until the mixture is light and fluffy, about 3 minutes. Scrape down the sides of the bowl with a rubber spatula. Add the vanilla, salt, and dulce de leche, and mix for 30 seconds on low speed.

With the mixer running on low speed, gradually add the confectioners' sugar, and then beat for 1 minute. Scrape down the bowl. If the filling is too soft to hold its shape, add more confectioners' sugar, a tablespoon at a time, until you reach the desired consistency.

Store in the refrigerator, in an airtight container with plastic wrap pressed onto the surface of the filling, for up to 5 days.

CHOCOLATE WHOOPIE PIES
with Peppermint Filling

Chocolate and mint get along like old chums. At the shop, we have a cookie that incorporates the two and when we describe it to customers, we are often met with a look of uncertainty. I think the skepticism comes from bad memories of a dessert flavored with "chewing gum" mint. When we explain that we use real peppermint extract, many people agree to give it a try. They are rarely disappointed that they did. The flavor of the natural extract is more comparable to sucking on a mint leaf than to taking a swig of Scope. We took the same flavor profile and used it in a whoopie pie. We liked what that did so much that we made it part of the holiday offering that year. It resulted in lots of Christmas cheer.

**MAKES 24
WHOOPIE PIES**

2 cups all-purpose flour

1/2 cup Dutch-processed cocoa powder

3/4 teaspoon baking soda

1/2 teaspoon table salt

1/2 cup granulated sugar

1/2 cup packed light brown sugar

1/2 cup plain whole-milk yogurt

1/3 cup canola oil

3 large eggs

1 teaspoon vanilla extract

Peppermint Filling (recipe follows)

1. In a medium bowl, whisk together the flour, cocoa powder, baking soda, and salt.

2. In the bowl of an electric mixer fitted with the paddle attachment, beat together the granulated sugar, brown sugar, yogurt, oil, eggs, and vanilla for 3 minutes on medium speed. Thoroughly scrape down the sides of the bowl with a rubber spatula. With the mixer running on low speed, gradually add the flour mixture for a total mixing time of 30 seconds. Carefully scrape down the bowl. Refrigerate the batter for 30 minutes.

3. Preheat the oven to 350°F. Line a baking sheet with parchment paper.

4. Using a pastry bag fitted with a large plain tip (the hole should be about as large as the tip of your ring finger), pipe 2-inch-diameter circles onto the prepared baking sheet, leaving 1½ inches between them. Be careful to keep your pastry bag completely vertical to achieve nice circles. (If you have to wait between batches of whoopie pies, keep the batter refrigerated.)

5. Immediately put the baking sheet in the oven. Bake for 9 minutes, without rotating the baking sheet, until the whoopie pies spring back when touched. Let the whoopie pies cool completely.

(recipe continues)

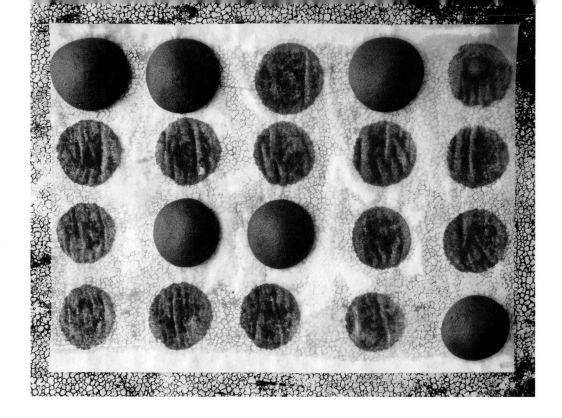

6. To fill the whoopies, turn half of them over so that they are bottom-side up. Using a pastry bag, pipe a small dollop of peppermint filling onto each whoopie bottom. Top with the remaining whoopies.

PEPPERMINT FILLING

MAKES 2 CUPS

4 ounces cream cheese, at room temperature

5 tablespoons unsalted butter, at room temperature

½ teaspoon peppermint extract

⅛ teaspoon table salt

3 cups confectioners' sugar, plus more if needed

In the bowl of an electric mixer fitted with the paddle attachment, beat together the cream cheese and butter on medium speed until the mixture is light and fluffy, about 3 minutes. Scrape down the sides of the bowl with a rubber spatula. Add the peppermint and salt, and mix for 30 seconds on low speed.

With the mixer running on low speed, gradually add the confectioners' sugar, and then beat for 1 minute. Scrape down the bowl. If the filling is too soft to hold its shape, add more confectioners' sugar, a tablespoon at a time, until you reach the desired consistency.

Store in the refrigerator, in an airtight container with plastic wrap pressed onto the surface of the filling, for up to 5 days.

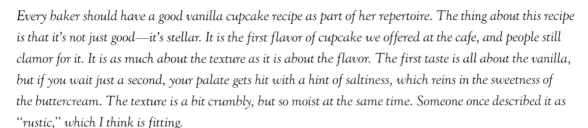

THE BEST VANILLA CUPCAKES
with Mocha Buttercream

Every baker should have a good vanilla cupcake recipe as part of her repertoire. The thing about this recipe is that it's not just good—it's stellar. It is the first flavor of cupcake we offered at the cafe, and people still clamor for it. It is as much about the texture as it is about the flavor. The first taste is all about the vanilla, but if you wait just a second, your palate gets hit with a hint of saltiness, which reins in the sweetness of the buttercream. The texture is a bit crumbly, but so moist at the same time. Someone once described it as "rustic," which I think is fitting.

As far as the buttercream is concerned, I am a sucker for anything that incorporates mocha. We used to pair this exclusively with chocolate cake, which is traditional and expected, but at One Girl, we like to throw in a surprise every now and then. It actually started when a regular customer placed an order for a birthday cake: vanilla cake with mocha buttercream. We were skeptical, but we are skeptics no more. It's an incredible combination. Dare I say, it's almost better than the chocolate.

MAKES 18 CUPCAKES

2 cups all-purpose flour

2 teaspoons baking powder

1½ teaspoons table salt

2 teaspoons vanilla extract

2 large egg whites

¾ cup whole milk

Pinch of table salt

12 tablespoons (1½ sticks) unsalted butter, at room temperature

1¾ cups sugar

Mocha Buttercream (recipe follows)

1. Preheat the oven to 350°F. Line one 12-cup muffin pan with paper liners and line 6 more cups in a second muffin tin.

2. In a medium bowl, whisk together the flour, baking powder, and salt.

3. In a large bowl, combine the vanilla, egg whites, milk, and salt. Whisk vigorously for 30 seconds.

4. In the bowl of an electric mixer fitted with the paddle attachment, beat together the butter and sugar on medium speed until light yellow and fluffy, about 3 minutes. Scrape down the sides of the bowl with a rubber spatula. With the mixer running on low speed, mix in a third of the flour mixture and half of the egg white mixture. Scrape down the bowl. Add another third of the flour mixture and all the remaining egg white mixture. Remove the bowl from the mixer, and using a rubber spatula, fold in the remaining flour mixture until all of the ingredients are fully incorporated.

(recipe continues)

TIP: This recipe calls for hot coffee in the mocha buttercream. Use the strongest brewed coffee you can find or, better yet, use espresso!

5. Using an ice cream scoop, divide the batter among the prepared muffin cups, filling them about three-fourths full.

6. Bake for 14 minutes. Then rotate the pan and bake for about 14 more minutes, or until a cake tester inserted in the center of one of the cupcakes comes out clean. Remove the pan from the oven and let the cupcakes cool in the pan for 20 minutes. Then remove the cupcakes from the pan, transfer them to a wire rack, and let them cool completely. Once the cupcakes are completely cool, frost them with the mocha buttercream.

MOCHA BUTTERCREAM

MAKES 4 CUPS

2 teaspoons instant coffee granules

¼ cup hot coffee or espresso (see Tip)

6 tablespoons whole milk, plus more if needed

1 tablespoon vanilla extract

12 tablespoons (1½ sticks) unsalted butter, at room temperature

½ teaspoon table salt

9 cups (2 pounds) confectioners' sugar

In a small bowl, dissolve the instant coffee granules in the hot coffee. Add the milk and vanilla, and stir to combine.

In the bowl of an electric mixer fitted with the paddle attachment, beat the butter on medium speed until it has begun to soften, about 3 minutes. Scrape down the sides of the bowl with a rubber spatula. With the mixer running on low speed, mix in the salt and half of the confectioners' sugar and all of the coffee mixture. Scrape down the bowl and the paddle. Add the remaining confectioners' sugar and mix for 2 minutes, until the buttercream is thoroughly combined. If the buttercream is too stiff to spread, add 1 to 2 teaspoons of milk, mixing for 10 seconds with each addition, until you reach the desired consistency.

Store in the refrigerator, in an airtight container with plastic wrap pressed onto the surface of the buttercream, for up to 5 days.

THE BEST CHOCOLATE CUPCAKES
with Vanilla Buttercream

The best? Yes, the best. I use that word confidently, and anyone who has had one of our chocolate cupcakes would more than likely agree. Chocolate cakes can sometimes be dry—an effect of the cocoa. But even though this recipe incorporates cocoa, it has some personality because it uses yogurt, as well as some unexpected techniques. The result is a super-moist cake that is really chocolatey but does not veer into fudgy territory—because it's a cake, after all!

For the buttercream, we prefer a traditional style as opposed to the more buttery Swiss meringue version. Ours will remind you of the dozens of cupcakes you enjoyed for classmates' birthday parties.

MAKES 18 CUPCAKES

¾ cups Dutch-processed cocoa powder

½ cup semisweet chocolate chips

½ cup plain whole-milk yogurt

1 teaspoon vanilla extract

1¼ cups all-purpose flour

1 teaspoon baking soda

½ teaspoon table salt

12 tablespoons (1½ sticks) unsalted butter, at room temperature

1 cup granulated sugar

½ cup packed light brown sugar

3 large eggs

Vanilla Buttercream (recipe follows)

1. Preheat the oven to 350°F. Line one 12-cup muffin pan with paper liners and line 6 more cups in a second muffin tin.

2. In a small saucepan, bring ¾ cup of water to a boil. In a medium heatproof bowl, combine the cocoa powder and the boiling water. Whisk vigorously until the cocoa has begun to dissolve into the water. Add the chocolate chips and continue to stir until the mixture is completely smooth, about 1 minute. Let it cool slightly. Then stir the yogurt and vanilla into the chocolate mixture.

3. In a medium bowl, whisk together the flour, baking soda, and salt.

4. In the bowl of an electric mixer fitted with the paddle attachment, beat together the butter, granulated sugar, and brown sugar on medium speed until light yellow and fluffy, about 3 minutes. Scrape down the sides of the bowl with a rubber spatula. With the mixer running on low speed, add the eggs one at a time. Mix for about 2 minutes, until fully combined. Scrape down the bowl again.

5. With the mixer running on low speed, mix in a third of the flour mixture and half of the chocolate mixture. Add another third of the flour mixture and all the remaining chocolate. Remove the bowl from the mixer, and use a rubber spatula to fold in the remaining flour mixture until all of the ingredients are fully incorporated.

6. Using an ice cream scoop, divide the batter among the prepared muffin cups, filling them about three-fourths full.

7. Bake for 15 minutes. Then rotate the pan and bake for about 15 more minutes, or until a cake tester inserted in the center of one of the cupcakes comes out clean. Remove the pan from the oven and let the cupcakes cool in the pan for 20 minutes. Then remove the cupcakes from the pan, transfer them to a wire rack, and let them cool completely.

8. Once the cupcakes are completely cool, frost them with the vanilla buttercream.

VANILLA BUTTERCREAM

MAKES 4 CUPS

2 pounds confectioners' sugar, plus more if needed

1 cup (2 sticks) unsalted butter, at room temperature

½ cup whole milk, plus more if needed

1 tablespoon vanilla extract

1 teaspoon table salt

In the bowl of an electric mixer fitted with the paddle attachment, beat together the butter and sugar on medium speed until the mixture is light yellow and fluffy, about 3 minutes. Scrape down the sides of the bowl with a rubber spatula.

With the mixer running on low speed, add the milk, vanilla, and salt. Scrape down the bowl and the paddle. Mix for 2 more minutes, until the buttercream is thoroughly combined. If the buttercream is too stiff to spread, add 1 to 2 teaspoons of milk, mixing for 10 seconds with each addition, until you reach the desired consistency.

Store in the refrigerator, in an airtight container with plastic wrap pressed onto the surface of the buttercream, for up to 5 days.

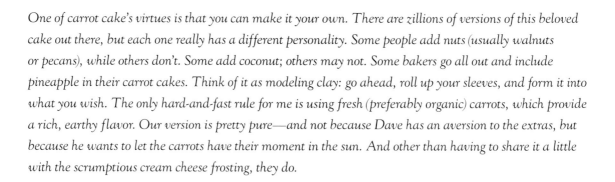

CARROT CUPCAKES
with Cream Cheese Frosting

One of carrot cake's virtues is that you can make it your own. There are zillions of versions of this beloved cake out there, but each one really has a different personality. Some people add nuts (usually walnuts or pecans), while others don't. Some add coconut; others may not. Some bakers go all out and include pineapple in their carrot cakes. Think of it as modeling clay: go ahead, roll up your sleeves, and form it into what you wish. The only hard-and-fast rule for me is using fresh (preferably organic) carrots, which provide a rich, earthy flavor. Our version is pretty pure—and not because Dave has an aversion to the extras, but because he wants to let the carrots have their moment in the sun. And other than having to share it a little with the scrumptious cream cheese frosting, they do.

MAKES 18 CUPCAKES

¾ cup chopped walnuts

½ cup granulated sugar

½ cup packed light brown sugar

2 large eggs

⅔ cup canola oil

½ pound carrots, peeled and shredded

6 tablespoons chopped crystallized ginger

½ cup golden raisins

1½ cups all-purpose flour

½ teaspoon baking powder

½ teaspoon baking soda

1 teaspoon ground cinnamon

½ teaspoon ground ginger

⅛ teaspoon ground nutmeg

1. Preheat the oven to 350°F. Line one 12-cup muffin pan with paper liners and line 6 more cups in a second muffin tin.

2. Spread the walnuts on a baking sheet, and toast them in the oven for 10 minutes, or until they are well browned and fragrant.

3. In the bowl of an electric mixer fitted with the paddle attachment, beat the granulated sugar, brown sugar, and eggs on low speed for 30 seconds. Increase the speed to medium-low and gradually add the oil. Scrape down the sides of the bowl, and mix for 2 more minutes. Add the shredded carrots, crystallized ginger, raisins, and walnuts. Mix on low speed for 30 seconds.

4. In a medium bowl, whisk together the flour, baking powder, baking soda, cinnamon, ground ginger, nutmeg, and salt. Add half of the flour mixture to the carrot mixture, and mix on low for 10 seconds. Scrape down the bowl and add the remaining flour mixture. Mix on low speed for 20 seconds. Scrape down the bowl again.

5. Using an ice cream scoop, divide the batter among the prepared muffin cups, filling them about three-fourths full.

¼ teaspoon table salt

Cream Cheese Frosting (page 69)

6. Bake for 14 minutes. Then rotate the pan and bake for about 14 more minutes, or until a cake tester inserted in the center of one of the cupcakes comes out clean. Remove the pan from the oven and let the cupcakes cool in the pan for 20 minutes. Then remove the cupcakes from the pan, transfer them to a wire rack, and let them cool completely. Once the cupcakes are completely cool, frost them with the cream cheese frosting.

Pies & Tarts

connie & florence, 1915, elmira, new york

NEW YORK STATE MAPLE PECAN PIE 94

APPLE PIE WITH A FLAKY BUTTER CRUST 97

FRESH PUMPKIN PIE WITH SALTY ROASTED PEPITAS 99

STRAWBERRY RHUBARB PIE WITH SPICED OAT CRUMBLE 102

FARM MARKET PLUM & MARZIPAN CROSTATA 105

MASCARPONE & FRESH FIG TART WITH A CORNMEAL CRUST 107

APRICOT, HONEY & PISTACHIO TART 110

ROSEMARY PEAR TART WITH AN ALMOND CRUST 112

NEW YORK STATE MAPLE PECAN PIE

Dave has a long-standing relationship with maple syrup. When he was a kid, his stepmom, Dee, would often prepare pancakes for Sunday breakfast. Pure maple syrup—nothing made in a factory by a fictional aunt—was the only accompaniment offered. Being a kid, that just wasn't sweet enough and he expressed this to his dad. Unfortunately, Bert didn't agree, so it was real maple syrup or nothing. Now, having a much more sophisticated palate, Dave would not dream of purchasing anything but pure syrup, preferably local, top grade. This recipe pairs that sweet syrup with chewy pecans in a delicious pie. Seems like his dad knew what he was talking about.

New York State produces some of the finest maple syrup out there. If by chance you do not live in New York, don't worry. There are many other places that produce maple syrup that is almost as good!

MAKES ONE 9-INCH PIE

CRUST

¼ cup rolled oats

1 tablespoon sugar

1¼ cups all-purpose flour

½ teaspoon table salt

8 tablespoons (1 stick) cold unsalted butter, cut into pieces

3 tablespoons ice water

1 large egg yolk

FILLING

1½ cups chopped unsalted pecans

3 large eggs

1 cup Grade B New York State maple syrup

4 tablespoons (½ stick) unsalted butter

½ cup sugar

1 teaspoon table salt

1. To make the crust, combine the oats and sugar in a food processor. Process for 2 minutes, or until the oats are a fine powder. Add the flour and salt, and pulse to combine. Add the butter and pulse 4 or 5 times, until the mixture resembles coarse crumbs. In a small bowl, stir together the ice water and egg yolk. Add the egg mixture to the food processor and pulse until the crumbs begin to climb the side of the bowl and hold their shape when pressed together. Turn the dough out onto a lightly floured work surface. Using your hands—and a little muscle—form the dough into a 5-inch disk. Wrap it in plastic wrap and refrigerate it for at least 1 hour or as long as 24 hours before rolling.

2. On a lightly floured work surface, use a rolling pin to roll the dough out into an 11-inch circle. Working quickly and carefully, line a 9-inch pie dish with the dough. With your fingertips, make sure that the edge of the pie is smooth and even. Refrigerate it for 20 minutes.

3. Preheat the oven to 350°F.

4. Remove the pie dish from the refrigerator. Line the crust with tin foil, making sure to cover the sides, and fill it with dried beans or pie weights. Bake for 15 minutes. Then rotate the crust and bake for

TIP: If you live in the southern United States, look for local pecans at your farmer's market. Here in the Northeast, you can certainly find local maple syrup to use in the recipe. For the maple syrup, use Grade B, or the darkest variety that you can find. It will impart the most maple flavor to your pie. Save the Grade A for pancakes!

another 15 minutes, or until the sides are somewhat firm and hold their shape. Remove the foil and weights, and bake for 6 minutes, or until the bottom of the crust looks dry and the shell is a very pale golden color. Remove the dish from the oven and let the crust cool while you make the filling. Leave the oven on.

5. To make the filling, spread the pecans out on a baking sheet and toast them in the oven for 8 minutes, or until they are brown and fragrant. Let the nuts cool for 10 minutes.

6. In a medium bowl, whisk together the eggs and maple syrup.

7. In a large heatproof bowl set over a pot of simmering water, melt the butter. Add the sugar and salt, and stir to combine. Add the egg mixture and stir gently until the syrup is hot to the touch. Remove the bowl from the top of the pan, and stir in the pecans. Pour the filling into the pie shell.

8. Bake for 15 minutes. Rotate the dish and bake for 20 more minutes, or until the filling is set in the middle. Transfer the dish to a wire rack and let the pie cool completely.

APPLE PIE
with a Flaky Butter Crust

To eat apple pie is to be American. Frankly, I think it should have a place in the Pledge of Allegiance. If I were to write the additional lines, I would feel obligated to specify "a really good" apple pie. What would constitute "really good"? Since there are only two major components—crust and apples—both need to be top-notch. A nicely formed, flaky crust is the foundation. In terms of apples, a range of flavors (some sweet, some tart) is the key. We always use New York State varieties, and we encourage you to buy ones that are indigenous to your area. Trying combinations of different types of apples and seeing which is your favorite is half the fun. Plus, that way you get to eat lots of pie in the name of research.

You should give this recipe a whirl, because it is a great one and apple pie is something every baker should have in his repertoire. To that end, Dave teaches a pie class at the shop each November. He always looks forward to the time when his students come back and, gleaming with pride, tell him how they impressed the whole family with their Thanksgiving pie.

MAKES ONE 9-INCH PIE

CRUST
2½ cups all-purpose flour

1½ tablespoons sugar

1 teaspoon table salt

1¼ cups (2½ sticks) cold unsalted butter, cut into pieces

4 to 5 tablespoons ice water

1. To make the crust, combine the flour, sugar, and salt in a food processor, and pulse to combine. Add the butter and pulse 4 or 5 times, until it is broken up into pea-sized pieces. Gradually add the ice water, pulsing until the mixture has a crumblike texture and is beginning to climb the sides of the bowl. Turn the dough out onto a lightly floured work surface. Using your hands—and a little muscle—form the dough into 2 equal 5-inch-diameter disks. Wrap them separately in plastic wrap, and refrigerate them for at least 1 hour or as long as 24 hours before rolling out.

2. To make the filling, peel, core, and quarter the apples. Then cut them into ¼-inch-thick slices. In a large bowl, combine the apples, sugar, lemon zest, lemon juice, salt, cinnamon, and nutmeg with a rubber spatula to coat them well. Let the mixture sit for 10 minutes, stirring them occasionally so that the apples will give off a bit of liquid.

3. Remove the dough from the refrigerator and unwrap one of the disks. Using a rolling pin, roll the dough out on a lightly floured work surface

(recipe continues)

5 or 6 medium apples

³/4 cup sugar

**¹/2 teaspoon grated
lemon zest**

**1 tablespoon fresh
lemon juice**

¹/4 teaspoon table salt

**¹/4 teaspoon ground
cinnamon**

**¹/4 teaspoon ground
nutmeg**

1 large egg white

1 tablespoon sugar

to form an 11-inch circle. Carefully transfer the circle to a 9-inch pie dish, allowing the excess dough to hang over the edge of the dish. Refrigerate the pie shell. Roll out the second disk of dough to form the top crust.

4. Scoop the apple filling into the pie shell, mounding it carefully so that none of the apples will pierce the top crust. Then carefully roll the dough for the top crust onto your rolling pin, and unroll it over the filling. Seal the edges of the pie by pinching the top crust over the bottom crust. Using a fork or your fingertips, make a decorative edge on the pie. (This will also help seal the dough.) Refrigerate the pie for 20 minutes.

5. Preheat the oven to 425°F.

6. Brush the top of the pie with the egg white, and then sprinkle the sugar on top. Using a very sharp paring knife, cut 3 to 5 vents through the top crust. This is an important step, as steam will need to escape as the pie bakes.

7. Put the pie dish on a rimmed baking sheet to catch any filling that drips over the side. Bake for 20 minutes, or until the top of the pie is a nice golden color. Reduce the oven temperature to 350°F and bake for 20 to 25 more minutes, until the filling begins to bubble up. Transfer the dish to a wire rack and let the pie cool completely.

FRESH PUMPKIN PIE
with Salty Roasted Pepitas

I love pumpkin pie so much that I've requested it as my birthday "cake" every year since I was about thirteen. I happen to have been born in October, so that helps my choice make some sense. I am also fortunate enough to be married to Dave, whom I refer to as a pie guru. The point is, I've eaten a lot of pumpkin pie, so I know what I'm talking about when I say that this is the best pumpkin pie ever. If someone feels otherwise, I am ready for a throwdown, because I can guarantee that their version does not have a grainy cornmeal crust and salty, crunchy pumpkin seeds on top. And without those elements, there's just no match.

MAKES ONE 9-INCH PIE

CRUST

1¼ cups all-purpose flour

¼ cup cornmeal

1 tablespoon sugar

½ teaspoon table salt

8 tablespoons (1 stick) cold unsalted butter, cut into pieces

3 tablespoons ice water

1 large egg yolk

PEPITAS

½ cup raw pumpkin seeds

½ teaspoon table salt

¼ teaspoon canola oil

1. To make the crust, combine the flour, cornmeal, sugar and salt in the bowl of a food processor and pulse to combine. Add the butter and pulse 4 or 5 times, until the mixture resembles coarse crumbs.

2. In a small bowl, mix together the ice water and egg yolk. Add the egg mixture to the food processor, and pulse until the crumbs begin to climb the side of the bowl and hold their shape when pressed together. Turn the dough out onto a lightly floured work surface. Using your hands—and a little muscle—form the dough into a 5-inch-diameter disk. Wrap it in plastic wrap and refrigerate it for at least 1 hour before rolling.

3. Unwrap the dough, and using a rolling pin, roll it out on a lightly floured work surface to form an 11-inch circle. Working quickly and carefully, line a 9-inch pie dish with the dough. With your fingertips, make sure that the edge of the pie is smooth and even. Refrigerate it for 20 minutes.

4. Preheat the oven to 350°F.

5. Remove the pie dish from the refrigerator. Line the crust with tin foil, making sure to cover the sides, and fill it with dried beans or pie weights. Bake for 15 minutes. Rotate the dish and bake for another

(recipe continues)

FILLING

1¹/₂ cups half-and-half

2 large eggs

1 15-ounce can pumpkin puree

³/₄ cup packed light brown sugar

1 teaspoon ground cinnamon

1 teaspoon ground ginger

¹/₂ teaspoon table salt

Pinch of ground cloves

15 minutes, or until the sides are somewhat firm and hold their shape. Remove the foil and bake for 6 minutes, until the bottom of the crust looks dry and the shell is a very pale golden color. Remove the dish from the oven and let the crust cool. Leave the oven on.

6. To make the pepitas, stir together the pumpkin seeds, salt, and oil in a small bowl. Scatter the seeds onto a small baking sheet and toast in the oven for 12 to 15 minutes, until the seeds are slightly toasted. Remove the baking sheet from the oven and let the pepitas cool.

7. To make the filling, mix together the half-and-half and eggs in a medium bowl. Add the pumpkin puree and mix well. Then add the brown sugar, cinnamon, ginger, salt, and cloves, and mix well. The filling will be very runny. Pour the filling into the pie shell. Sprinkle the pepitas on the filling.

8. Bake for 25 minutes. Rotate the dish and bake for 20 more minutes, or until the center of the pie jiggles just a bit when you touch the oven rack. Transfer the dish to a wire rack and let the pie cool completely.

STRAWBERRY RHUBARB PIE
with Spiced Oat Crumble

If this pie could speak, it would say this to winter: "Thanks for visiting. Don't let the door hit you on the way out." After three or four long, cold months in New York, strawberries and rhubarb are two of the first signs of spring to appear at the market, and they are a welcome sight. They represent the beginning of sun-soaked days, outdoor grilling, and plenty of fresh fruits and vegetables. Since I'm not a big fan of the cold, this pie makes me feel utterly elated and excited about what the coming months hold.

You don't often find strawberry recipes that incorporate the spices that are usually reserved for fall desserts, but you'll be pleasantly surprised by how well the berries get along with the likes of nutmeg and ginger. I think rhubarb is such a rock star that I have experimented with omitting the strawberries altogether. But the mix of berries and rhubarb—plus a great oat crumb topping—will surely get you a standing ovation.

MAKES ONE 9-INCH PIE

CRUST

1 cup all-purpose flour

¼ cup whole wheat flour

1 tablespoon granulated sugar

½ teaspoon table salt

10 tablespoons (1¼ sticks) cold unsalted butter, cut into pieces

3 tablespoons ice water

FILLING

3 cups sliced hulled strawberries

3 cups sliced rhubarb

½ cup granulated sugar

2 teaspoons grated orange zest

2 teaspoons fresh lemon juice

1. To make the crust, combine the flours, sugar, and salt in a food processor, and pulse to combine. Add the butter and pulse 4 or 5 times, until it is broken up into pea-sized pieces. Gradually add the ice water, pulsing until the mixture has a crumblike texture and is beginning to climb the sides of the bowl. Turn the dough out onto a lightly floured work surface. Using your hands—and a little muscle—form the dough into a 5-inch-diameter disk. Wrap it in plastic wrap, and refrigerate it for at least 1 hour or as long as 24 hours before rolling.

2. On a lightly floured work surface, use a rolling pin to roll the dough out into an 11-inch circle. Working quickly and carefully, line a 9-inch pie dish with the dough. With your fingertips, make sure that the edge of the pie is smooth and even. Refrigerate the crust while you prepare the other elements.

3. To make the filling, combine the strawberries, rhubarb, sugar, orange zest, lemon juice, vanilla, and tapioca in a large bowl. Stir to combine. Let rest at room temperature for 10 minutes.

¼ teaspoon vanilla
extract

3 tablespoons instant
tapioca (see Tip)

TOPPING

¾ cup all-purpose flour

½ cup packed light brown
sugar

½ teaspoon ground
ginger

⅛ teaspoon ground
nutmeg

½ cup rolled oats

¼ cup minced crystallized
ginger

½ teaspoon table salt

10 tablespoons (1¼ sticks)
cold unsalted butter, cut
into pieces

1 teaspoon whole milk

1 tablespoon granulated
sugar

TIP: Tapioca can be found
in the supermarket, near
the gelatin and Jell-O.

4. To make the topping, combine the flour, brown sugar, ground ginger, nutmeg, oats, crystallized ginger, and salt in the bowl of a food processor. Pulse to combine. Add the butter and pulse until the mixture is well blended and resembles coarse crumbs.

5. Preheat the oven to 400°F.

6. Scoop the filling into the cold pie crust. Then mound the crumb topping over the filling. With a pastry brush, brush the milk over the edge of the pie crust. Sprinkle the sugar over the crust. Put the pie dish on a rimmed baking sheet to catch any filling that drips over the side.

7. Bake for 10 minutes, or until the crust is a nice golden color. Reduce the oven temperature to 350°F and bake for 20 to 25 more minutes, until the filling begins to bubble up. Transfer the dish to a wire rack and let the pie cool completely.

FARM MARKET PLUM & MARZIPAN CROSTATA

On this side of the Atlantic, marzipan is one of those ingredients that cannot get a fair shake. In Sicily, on the other hand, the windows of many pasticcerie (pastry shops) boast an artful display of beautiful little marzipan figurines, usually in the form of brightly colored fruits and vegetables. As an art form that Sicilians take very seriously, they are quite lovely to look at, although eating them might be considered almond paste overload. But since Sicilians use marzipan with a liberal hand in many cookies and desserts, there are plenty of other ways to taste this traditional sweet. It definitely has a very distinct flavor, and poor-quality almond paste has an off-putting perfumey taste. Seek out the good stuff, which thankfully can be found in most specialty food stores. Married here with tart plums (not surprisingly, I think the Italian prune plums are the best choice), the marzipan is counterbalanced and made irresistible.

MAKES ONE 8-INCH CROSTATA

CRUST

1¹⁄₂ cups all-purpose flour

1 tablespoon sugar

¹⁄₂ teaspoon table salt

8 tablespoons (1 stick) cold unsalted butter, cut into pieces

3 tablespoons ice water

1 large egg yolk

1. To make the crust, combine the flour, sugar, and salt in a food processor, and pulse to combine. Add the butter and pulse 4 or 5 times, until the mixture resembles coarse crumbs. In a small bowl, mix together the ice water and egg yolk. Add the egg mixture to the food processor, and pulse until the crumbs begin to climb the sides of the bowl and hold their shape when pressed together. Turn the dough out onto a lightly floured work surface. Using your hands—and a little muscle—form the dough into a 5-inch-diameter disk. Wrap it in plastic wrap and refrigerate it for at least 1 hour or as long as 24 hours before rolling.

2. To make the filling, cut the plums in half and remove the pits. Depending on the size of the plums, cut each half into 2 or 3 wedges—the skin side of each wedge should be about as thick as your finger.

3. Preheat the oven to 425°F. Line a baking sheet with parchment paper.

4. Unwrap the dough, and using a rolling pin, roll it out on a lightly floured work surface to form an 11-inch circle. With your fingertips,

(recipe continues)

1½ pounds firm ripe plums

½ cup almond paste

¼ cup sugar

¼ teaspoon table salt

1 large egg

4 tablespoons (½ stick) unsalted butter, at room temperature

2 tablespoons all-purpose flour

1 large egg yolk

1 tablespoon heavy cream

2 teaspoons sugar

make sure that the edge of the crust is smooth and even. Working quickly and carefully, roll the dough back up onto the rolling pin, and then unroll it onto the prepared baking sheet.

5. In a medium bowl, combine the almond paste, sugar, salt, and egg. Mix well with a rubber spatula. Add the butter and flour, and mix thoroughly. Spread the almond paste mixture over the round of dough, leaving a 3½-inch border. Arrange the sliced plums over the filling. Carefully fold the edge of the crust up and over the filling and plums, leaving the center of the tart open.

6. Mix the egg yolk with the heavy cream in a small bowl. Using a pastry brush, brush this egg wash over the crust. Sprinkle the sugar over the egg wash.

7. Bake for 15 minutes. Rotate the baking sheet and reduce the room temperature to 350°F. Bake for 20 more minutes, or until the crust is golden and the filling has puffed up and is a soft golden color. Transfer the baking sheet to a wire rack and let the crostata cool completely.

8. When it has cooled, slide a thin metal spatula under the crust to separate it from the parchment paper, and carefully slide the crostata onto a serving plate.

MASCARPONE & FRESH FIG TART
with a Cornmeal Crust

I have a love affair with figs. Black or white, dried or fresh, I can't get enough. The fact that my grandfather grew a fig tree in his itsy-bitsy backyard in Queens, New York, might have something to do with my obsession. This might not be strange to many Italian Americans who grew up with a fig tree in their yard, right next to the basil plants. But I am willing to bet that most people think it unusual to endeavor to grow anything you might eat in the soil of New York City. I guess you can say Papa was one of the city's original urban farmers. And my affinity for figs is the result. When Dave came up with this recipe, I would've agreed to marry him on the spot if we hadn't already been married. It's imperative to buy the figs when they are in season, which is usually twice a year, when they are at their sweetest. When they are teamed up with the coarse texture of the cornmeal and the creaminess of the mascarpone, it's a home run.

MAKES ONE 9-INCH TART

CRUST

1¼ cups all-purpose flour

¼ cup cornmeal

2 tablespoons sugar

½ teaspoon table salt

8 tablespoons (1 stick) cold unsalted butter, cut into pieces

3 tablespoons ice water

1 large egg yolk

FILLING

1 cup mascarpone cheese

2/3 cup sour cream

½ cup honey

1 teaspoon vanilla extract

8 to 12 fresh figs, halved (see Tip)

1. To make the crust, combine the flour, cornmeal, sugar, and salt in a food processor and pulse to combine. Add the butter and pulse 4 or 5 times, until the mixture resembles coarse crumbs. In a small bowl, stir together the ice water and egg yolk. Add the egg mixture to the food processor and pulse until the crumbs begin to climb the side of the bowl and hold their shape when pressed together. Turn the dough out onto a work surface. Using your hands—and a little muscle—form the dough into a 5-inch-diameter disk. Wrap it in plastic wrap and refrigerate it for at least 1 hour or as long as 24 hours before rolling.

2. Unwrap the dough, and using a rolling pin, roll it out on a lightly floured work surface to form an 11-inch circle. Working quickly and carefully, line a 9-inch tart pan with the dough. With your fingertips, make sure that the edge of the tart is smooth and even. Refrigerate it for 20 minutes.

3. Preheat the oven to 350°F.

4. Remove the tart pan from the refrigerator. Line the crust with tin foil, making sure to cover the sides, and fill it with dried beans or pie

(recipe continues)

TIP: Figs can vary a great deal in size. It is most important to look for plump, good-looking figs.

weights. Bake for 15 minutes. Rotate the pan and bake for 15 more minutes, or until the sides are somewhat firm and hold their shape. Remove the foil and bake for 6 minutes, or until the bottom of the crust looks dry and the shell is a very pale golden color. Remove the pan from the oven and let the shell cool.

5. To make the filling, beat together the mascarpone and sour cream in the bowl of an electric mixer fitted with the paddle attachment. Then beat on medium speed for 1 minute. Scrape down the sides of the bowl with a rubber spatula. Add the honey and vanilla, and mix on medium speed for 30 seconds.

6. When the crust is cool, spread the filling evenly in the bottom. Arrange the figs, cut side up, in a circular pattern on top of the filling. The tart will keep in an airtight container in the refrigerator for up to 2 days, but it is best when eaten the same day it is assembled.

APRICOT, HONEY & PISTACHIO TART

A frangipane base is hands down, without a doubt, my favorite tart technique. Frangipane is a type of pastry cream, usually made with nuts, and for this tart we use pistachios. This method of tart making involves placing the fruit in the frangipane so that while it is baking, it becomes embedded in the filling. I cannot think of anything more delicious than being immersed in pistachio frangipane. This tart features sweet caramelized apricots surrounded by a slightly crunchy pastry cream, covering a somewhat chewy center. Yes, beautiful and delicious.

MAKES ONE
10-INCH TART

CRUST

1½ cups all-purpose flour

1 tablespoon sugar

½ teaspoon table salt

8 tablespoons (1 stick) cold unsalted butter, cut into pieces

3 tablespoons ice water

1 large egg yolk

FRANGIPANE FILLING

½ cup shelled unsalted pistachios

¼ cup sugar

½ teaspoon grated lemon zest

6 tablespoons (¾ stick) unsalted butter, at room temperature

1 large egg

¼ cup honey

6 ripe medium apricots, pitted and quartered

1 teaspoon whole milk

1 teaspoon sugar

1. To make the crust, in the bowl of a food processor, combine the flour, sugar, and salt. Pulse to combine. Add the butter and pulse 4 or 5 times, until the mixture resembles coarse crumbs. In a small bowl, stir together the ice water and egg yolk. Add the egg mixture, and pulse until the crumbs begin to climb the side of the bowl and hold their shape when pressed together. Turn the dough out onto a work surface. Using your hands—and a little muscle—form the dough into a 5-inch-diameter disk. Wrap it in plastic wrap and refrigerate it for at least 1 hour or as long as 24 hours before rolling.

2. Unwrap the dough, and using a rolling pin, roll it out on a lightly floured work surface to form a 12-inch circle. Working quickly and carefully, line a 10-inch tart pan with the dough. With your fingertips, make sure that the edge of the tart is smooth and even. Refrigerate it for 20 minutes.

3. To make the filling, combine the pistachios and sugar in a food processor, and process for 1 minute. Add the lemon zest and butter, and pulse until all of the butter has been incorporated and the mixture resembles coarse crumbs. Add the egg and pulse 2 or 3 times, until the frangipane filling is fully mixed.

4. Preheat the oven to 350°F.

5. To assemble the tart, spread the frangipane filling over the bottom of the crust. Drizzle the honey over the frangipane. Arrange the apricot

quarters on top. Using a pastry brush, brush the milk around the edge of the crust. Then sprinkle with the sugar. Transfer the tart pan to a rimmed baking sheet to catch any filling that may drip over the side.

6. Bake for 25 minutes. Rotate the pan and bake for 25 more minutes, or until the filling is a nice golden color and has puffed up a bit over the apricots. Transfer the pan to a wire rack and let the tart cool completely.

ROSEMARY PEAR TART
with an Almond Crust

As much as I love the crunch of a raw pear, I think it is one of the few fruits that actually improves with baking. There is a latent sweetness that emerges once the fruit comes into contact with heat. I liken the raw pear to a woman wearing her hair in a tight bun, her long locks let down and her true personality emerging with a little bit of cooking. We invited almonds and rosemary along for the adventure. They are flavorful participants that really bring out the best in the pears. The only improvement I can think of for a slice of this tart . . . is a second slice.

MAKES ONE 9-INCH TART

CRUST

½ cup sliced almonds

1¼ cups all-purpose flour

1 tablespoon sugar

½ teaspoon table salt

8 tablespoons (1 stick) cold unsalted butter, cut into pieces

3 tablespoons ice water

1 large egg yolk

TOPPING

¾ cup sugar

¾ cup all-purpose flour

⅛ teaspoon table salt

Pinch of ground nutmeg

6 tablespoons (¾ stick) unsalted butter, melted

1. To make the crust, spread the almonds out on a baking sheet, and toast them in the oven for 5 minutes, or until they are just starting to turn golden. Let the almonds cool.

2. Transfer the almonds to a food processor, and pulse until they are fine and powdery. Add the flour, sugar, and salt, and pulse to mix. Then add the butter and pulse 4 or 5 times, until the mixture resembles coarse crumbs. In a small bowl, mix together the ice water and egg yolk. Add the egg mixture to the food processor, and pulse until the crumbs begin to climb the sides of the bowl and hold their shape when pressed together. Turn the dough out onto a lightly floured work surface. Using your hands—and a little muscle—form the dough into a 5-inch-diameter disk. Wrap it in plastic wrap and refrigerate it for at least 1 hour and as long as 24 hours before rolling.

3. Unwrap the dough, and using a rolling pin, roll it out on a lightly floured work surface to form an 11-inch circle. Working quickly and carefully, line a 9-inch tart pan with the dough. With your fingertips, make sure that the edge of the tart is smooth and even. Refrigerate it for 20 minutes.

4. Preheat the oven to 350°F.

5. Remove the tart pan from the refrigerator. Line the crust with tin foil, making sure to cover the sides, and fill it with dried beans or pie

FILLING

2 egg yolks

2 tablespoons honey

1 tablespoon sugar

1/2 teaspoon table salt

3/4 cup mascarpone cheese

2 teaspoons chopped fresh rosemary leaves

PEARS

1 teaspoon fresh lemon juice

3 firm Bosc pears

weights. Bake for 15 minutes. Rotate the pan and bake for 15 more minutes, or until the sides are somewhat firm and hold their shape. Remove the foil and bake for 6 minutes, or until the bottom of the crust looks dry and the shell is a very pale golden color. Remove the pan from the oven and let the shell cool.

6. To make the topping, combine the sugar, flour, salt, and nutmeg in a medium bowl. Add the melted butter and mix thoroughly.

7. To make the filling, combine the egg yolks, honey, sugar, and salt in a small bowl. Stir in the mascarpone and rosemary.

8. To prepare the pears, add the lemon juice to a bowl of cold water. Peel, halve, and core the pears. As you work, submerge the peeled pear halves in the acidulated water to prevent them from browning.

9. To assemble the tart, spread the filling mixture evenly over the bottom of the crust. Drain the pears and thinly slice them. Arrange the pear slices over the filling. Sprinkle the crumb topping over the pears.

10. Bake the tart for 25 minutes. Rotate the pan and bake for 20 more minutes. Transfer the pan to a wire rack and let the tart cool completely.

Breakfast

aunt lillian, poppy & dad, 1943, bronx, new york

CURRANT YOGURT SCONES

Brunch is one of our favorite meals to host at our home. It works for friends who have kids and those who don't, people who eat meat and those who refrain, and so on. In other words, it's the meal for all people. That being said, we are often challenged to come up with new brunch items to add to our repertoire. Dave devised this scone recipe for a Mother's Day brunch, and everyone agreed that the added texture from the oats was pretty outstanding. We included them in a menu of banana pancakes, baked eggs, Niçoise salad, and leeks vinaigrette. I would venture to say that it may have been one of the best Mother's Day meals the moms had, and we cannot underestimate these scones' role in that.

MAKES 8 SCONES

1 cup rolled oats

¾ cup all-purpose flour

½ cup whole wheat flour

⅓ cup sugar

1½ teaspoons baking powder

1 teaspoon baking soda

1 teaspoon table salt

10 tablespoons (1¼ sticks) cold unsalted butter, cut into pieces

1 large egg

½ cup plain whole-milk yogurt

½ cup dried currants

1 large egg yolk

1 tablespoon whole milk

Turbinado sugar

1. Preheat the oven to 400°F.

2. In the bowl of a food processor, combine the oats, the flours, sugar, baking powder, baking soda, and salt. Pulse to combine. Add the butter and pulse 4 or 5 times, until it is broken up into pea-sized pieces. Pour the mixture into a large bowl.

3. In a small bowl, mix together the egg and yogurt. Using a rubber spatula, fold the egg mixture and the currants into the flour mixture. At this point the dough should be very sticky.

4. Turn the dough out onto a lightly floured work surface. Flour your hands, and pat the dough into an 8-inch circle. Let the dough rest for 5 minutes. Then, using a large chef's knife, cut the circle into 8 wedges. Transfer the wedges to a parchment paper–lined baking sheet.

5. In a small bowl, stir the egg yolk and milk together with a fork. Brush the scones lightly with this egg wash, and sprinkle them generously with turbinado sugar.

6. Place the baking sheet in the oven and reduce the temperature to 350°F. Bake the scones for 14 minutes. Rotate the baking sheet, and bake for 12 to 14 more minutes, until the tops of the scones are a light golden color. Transfer the scones to a wire rack and let them cool completely.

LEMON SCONES

When Dave first moved to the scary Big Apple, he would always find comfort at his sister Lynne's apartment on West 15th Street. There his brother-in-law would whip up all sorts of delicious comfort food. Some nights the menu would consist of a roast or maybe macaroni and cheese. On weekends, Dave typically visited them for brunch, and these scones almost always made the cut. Because they were better than any scone he had eaten before, Dave says that they were his first introduction to "real" scones and their proper preparation. These are flaky and light and we recommend making them often—it would be criminal to save them only for Sundays. Enjoy them with a touch of homemade butter (page 129) and your favorite preserves.

MAKES 8 SCONES

3 cups all-purpose flour

1/2 cup sugar

2 teaspoons baking powder

1/2 teaspoon baking soda

1/2 teaspoon table salt

12 tablespoons (1 1/2 sticks) cold unsalted butter, cut into pieces

1 cup buttermilk

Grated zest of 2 lemons

1/4 cup heavy cream

Turbinado sugar

TIPS: Scones freeze very well after they have been cut. Wrap them tightly in plastic wrap, and freeze for a month or so. Simply take them out of the freezer, brush with cream, sprinkle with sugar, and bake as instructed, adding 4 minutes to the total baking time.

1. Preheat the oven to 400°F.

2. In the bowl of a food processor, combine the flour, sugar, baking powder, baking soda, and salt. Pulse to combine. Add the butter and pulse 4 or 5 times, until the butter is broken up into pea-sized pieces. Pour the mixture into a large bowl.

3. In a separate bowl, mix together the buttermilk and lemon zest. Using a rubber spatula, fold the buttermilk mixture into the flour mixture. At this point the dough should be very sticky.

4. Turn the dough out onto a lightly floured work surface. Flour your hands, and pat the dough into an 8-inch circle. Let the dough rest for 5 minutes. Then, using a large chef's knife, cut the circle into 8 wedges. Transfer the wedges to a parchment paper–lined baking sheet. Brush the tops of the scones lightly with the heavy cream, and sprinkle them generously with turbinado sugar.

5. Place the baking sheet in the oven and reduce the temperature to 350°F. Bake the scones for 10 minutes. Rotate the baking sheet, and bake for 8 to 10 more minutes, until the tops of the scones are a light golden color. Transfer the scones to a wire rack to cool.

HONEY APRICOT GRANOLA

We get requests for all sorts of things here at the shop. One of our regular customers who has been coming in since day one is a huge fan of our granola. She also happens to adore dried apricots. She was so determined to get Dave to come up with an apricot granola that he finally caved and fulfilled her wish. What he created was a crunchy, slightly sweet blend that includes almonds, coconut, and sunflower seeds . . . and of course a healthy portion of dried apricots. Well, we were all smitten. That customer knew what she was talking about.

MAKES 7½ CUPS

4½ cups old-fashioned rolled oats

1 cup slivered almonds

½ cup unsalted sunflower seeds

½ cup unsweetened shredded coconut

½ teaspoon table salt

½ cup honey

¼ cup canola oil

1½ teaspoons vanilla extract

¾ cup dried apricots, chopped

1. Preheat the oven to 350°F.

2. Spread the oats out on two baking sheets, and toast them in the oven for 14 minutes. Then transfer them to a very large bowl and let them cool.

3. On a baking sheet, toast each of the following ingredients separately: the almonds for 10 minutes, the sunflower seeds for 8 minutes, and the coconut for just 1 minute. Add the toasted nuts and coconut to the oats, and stir. Reduce the oven temperature to 225°F.

4. Add the salt, honey, oil, and vanilla to the mixture in the bowl, and mix thoroughly. Divide the mixture between the two baking sheets, and bake for 2 hours. Remove the baking sheets from the oven and let the granola cool for 20 minutes.

5. In a large bowl, combine the apricots with the baked ingredients. Allow the granola to cool to room temperature. The granola will keep in an airtight container for up to 2 weeks.

VARIATION

If you would like to increase your granola repertoire, try this variation: Substitute ½ cup sliced almonds, ½ cup walnut pieces, and ½ cup raw pumpkin seeds for the almonds and sunflower seeds. Then substitute ½ cup maple syrup for the honey. Finally, add ½ cup dried currants and ½ dried cranberries for the dried apricots. Prepare the granola according to the recipe above.

STEWED FRUIT

Our friend Robert deserves credit for this recipe, which is our favorite accompaniment to our homemade yogurt (page 130). He was the first person to suggest stewing the fruit rather than leaving it raw. We had been so accustomed to eating it uncooked that we had no idea what potential the fruit held. What a revelation! The light cooking draws out the natural sweetness, and it provides an opportunity to add another dimension of flavor with some spices. It's especially good in the colder months, when great-tasting fresh fruit is harder to come by.

MAKES 2½ CUPS

1 lemon

5 medium pears, apples, nectarines, plums, or apricots

1½ cups sugar

1 cinnamon stick

1. With a vegetable peeler, peel long ½-inch-wide strips of zest from the lemon. If there is any pith attached to the zest, remove it with a paring knife. Juice the lemon into a large bowl.

2. If you are using pears or apples, peel, halve, core, and slice them into ¼-inch-wide wedges. If you are using nectarines, plums, or apricots, halve and pit the fruit, and cut it into ¼-inch-wide wedges. Add the fruit to the lemon juice, and pour in enough cool water to cover.

3. In a medium pot set over medium-high heat, bring 4 cups of water and the sugar to a gentle simmer. Stir in the cinnamon stick and lemon zest. Cook for 3 minutes.

4. Drain the fruit, add it to the pot, and cook for 2 minutes. Remove the pan from the heat, and let the fruit come to room temperature in the liquid. Discard the zest and the cinnamon stick. The stewed fruit can be stored in an airtight container in the refrigerator for up to 2 weeks.

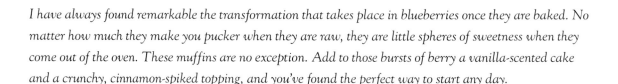

BLUEBERRY OAT MUFFINS
with Crumb Topping

I have always found remarkable the transformation that takes place in blueberries once they are baked. No matter how much they make you pucker when they are raw, they are little spheres of sweetness when they come out of the oven. These muffins are no exception. Add to those bursts of berry a vanilla-scented cake and a crunchy, cinnamon-spiked topping, and you've found the perfect way to start any day.

MAKES 12 MUFFINS

CRUMB TOPPING

1 cup all-purpose flour

1/2 cup packed light brown sugar

1/4 cup rolled oats

1/2 teaspoon ground cinnamon

1/4 teaspoon table salt

10 tablespoons (1 1/4 sticks) cold unsalted butter, cut into pieces

MUFFINS

2/3 cup rolled oats

2 cups all-purpose flour

1 teaspoon baking powder

1/2 teaspoon baking soda

1 1/2 teaspoons table salt

6 tablespoons (3/4 stick) unsalted butter, at room temperature

1 cup granulated sugar

2 large eggs

1 cup sour cream

1/4 cup honey

1 teaspoon vanilla extract

2 cups frozen blueberries

1. Preheat the oven to 350°F. Line one 12-cup muffin pan with paper liners.

2. To prepare the crumb topping, combine the flour, brown sugar, oats, cinnamon, and salt in the bowl of a food processor, and pulse to combine. Add the butter and pulse 4 or 5 times. Set aside.

3. To prepare the muffins, process the oats in the clean bowl of the food processor until they are powdery. In a medium bowl, whisk together the ground oats, flour, baking powder, baking soda, and salt.

4. In the bowl of an electric mixer fitted with the paddle attachment, beat together the butter and granulated sugar on medium speed until light yellow and fluffy, about 3 minutes. Add the eggs one at a time, and mix for 1 minute. Then add the sour cream, honey, and vanilla, and mix for 30 seconds. With the mixer running on low speed, gradually add the flour mixture. Mix for 10 seconds. Take the bowl off the mixer and fold in the blueberries with a rubber spatula.

5. Using an ice cream scoop, divide the batter among the prepared muffin cups, filling them about three-fourths full. Sprinkle the muffins generously with the crumb topping.

6. Bake, rotating the pan halfway through, for 28 minutes, or until the top of a muffin springs back when lightly pressed. Let the muffins cool in the pan for 10 minutes. Remove the muffins from the pan, transfer them to a wire rack, and let them cool completely.

BANANA WALNUT MUFFINS

We have all had the experience of eating a gummy banana muffin—it can be like munching on caulk. Well, we'll have none of that here. This muffin has a great cakey texture (but not too sweet, like cake) and crunchy walnuts to boot. I should mention that I think an integral part of proper consumption involves a healthy schmear of cream cheese.

MAKES 12 MUFFINS

1½ cups chopped walnuts

1 pound ripe bananas

½ teaspoon fresh lemon juice

8 tablespoons (1 stick) unsalted butter, at room temperature

1½ cups sugar

3 large eggs

2¼ cups all-purpose flour

2 teaspoons baking powder

1 teaspoon baking soda

½ teaspoon table salt

½ cup buttermilk

1 teaspoon vanilla extract

1. Preheat the oven to 350°F. Line one 12-cup muffin pan with paper liners.

2. Put the walnuts on a baking sheet and toast them in the oven for 15 minutes. Let cool for 10 minutes.

3. Combine the bananas and lemon juice in a food processor, and process until pureed.

4. In the bowl of an electric mixer fitted with the paddle attachment, beat together the butter and sugar on medium speed until the mixture is light yellow and fluffy, about 3 minutes. Scrape down the sides of the bowl with a rubber spatula. With the mixer running on low speed, add the eggs one at a time. Mix for about 2 minutes, until fully combined. Scrape down the bowl again. Add the banana puree and mix for 30 seconds.

5. In a medium bowl, whisk together the flour, baking powder, baking soda, and salt. In a separate bowl, combine the buttermilk and vanilla. With the mixer running on low speed, mix in a third of the flour mixture and half of the buttermilk mixture. Add another third of the flour mixture and all the remaining buttermilk mixture. Using a rubber spatula, fold in the remaining flour mixture and the walnuts.

6. Using an ice cream scoop, divide the batter among the prepared muffin cups, filling them about three-fourths full. Bake, rotating the pan halfway through, for 28 minutes, or until the top of a muffin springs back when lightly pressed. Let the muffins cool in the pan for 10 minutes. Remove the muffins from the pan, transfer them to a wire rack, and let them cool completely.

MULTIGRAIN MUFFINS

Healthy food that tastes delicious—isn't that what everyone wants? The culinary landscape of America has changed so much in recent years that it has never been easier to reach that goal. The local, sustainable, seasonal, farm-to-table movement has basically barged into our homes and plopped gorgeous, fresh, healthy fruits and vegetables on our tables. This is something that makes me utterly happy. These muffins are edible nuggets of that philosophy. When Dave makes them here, he uses cornmeal that is ground in Rhinebeck, New York, the town we got married in. To that, he adds applesauce that he makes from New York State apples, plus some local oats. How's that for healthy and local?

MAKES 12 MUFFINS

1 cup old-fashioned rolled oats

2 cups all-purpose flour

1 cup cornmeal

1/2 cup whole wheat flour

1 1/2 teaspoons baking powder

1 teaspoon baking soda

1 teaspoon salt

3/4 cup packed light brown sugar

2 eggs

8 tablespoons (1 stick) unsalted butter, melted

3/4 cup sour cream

3/4 cup applesauce

1/2 cup plain whole-milk yogurt

1/4 cup honey

1/2 cup unsalted sunflower seeds

Granulated sugar, for dusting

1. Preheat the oven to 350°F. Line one 12-cup muffin pan with paper liners.

2. In a food processor, grind the oats until they are powdery. Add the flour, cornmeal, whole wheat flour, baking powder, baking soda, and salt. Pulse 2 to 3 times to combine. Set aside.

3. In the bowl of an electric mixer fitted with the paddle attachment, beat together the brown sugar and eggs on medium speed for 1 minute. Scrape down the bowl with a rubber spatula. Add the melted butter and mix on medium speed for 30 seconds. Add the sour cream, applesauce, yogurt, and honey and mix on medium speed for 30 seconds. Scrape down the bowl with a rubber spatula. With the mixer running on low speed, add the flour mixture and mix for 20 seconds.

4. Using an ice-cream scoop, divide the batter among the prepared muffin cups, filling them about three-fourths full. Sprinkle the muffins with the sunflower seeds and sprinkle with sugar. Bake for 14 minutes. Rotate the pan and bake for about 14 more minutes, or until the tops of the muffins spring back when lightly pressed. Remove the pan from the oven and let the muffins cool for 10 minutes. Remove the muffins from the pan and transfer them to a wire rack to cool completely.

BUTTERMILK BISCUITS

The buttermilk in biscuit recipes is there to ensure a truly flaky biscuit. This is a fortunate thing for us because we happen to have lots of buttermilk on hand. Why is that? It's because we put such care into the details that we make our own butter for breakfast (see page 129). We are very proud of this, but what it means is that after we offer a delicious topping for our freshly made baked goods, we end up with an abundance of buttermilk. Dave set out to find creative uses for it, and these biscuits are the fortunate result. He experimented with replacing the milk in his favorite biscuit recipe with buttermilk, and what he got was an incredibly flaky biscuit with a moist center and crunchy baked exterior. Ironically, these biscuits don't really need the butter that was responsible for their creation!

**MAKES ABOUT
8 BISCUITS**

2 cups all-purpose flour

1 tablespoon baking powder

½ teaspoon table salt

4 tablespoons (½ stick) cold unsalted butter, cut into pieces

¾ cup buttermilk

1 large egg yolk

1 tablespoon whole milk

1. Preheat the oven to 350°F.

2. In the bowl of a food processor, combine the flour, baking powder, and salt. Pulse to combine. Add the butter and pulse 4 or 5 times, until it is broken up into pea-sized pieces. Pour in half of the buttermilk and pulse once. Add the remaining buttermilk and pulse 3 times to combine. The dough should start to gather around the blade of the food processor.

3. Turn the dough out onto a lightly floured work surface. Flour your hands, and pat the dough into a 1-inch-thick circle. Using a 3-inch round biscuit cutter, cut out as many biscuits as you can. Place the biscuits on a parchment paper–lined baking sheet, spaced about an inch apart. Gently reshape the remaining dough, and once again cut out as many biscuits as possible. Add them to the baking sheet.

4. In a small bowl, stir the egg yolk and milk together with a fork. Brush the biscuits lightly with this egg wash.

5. Bake the biscuits for 10 minutes. Rotate the baking sheet and bake for 8 to 10 more minutes, until both the tops and the bottoms of the biscuits are a rich golden color. Transfer the biscuits to a wire rack and let them cool for 5 minutes before serving.

FARMSTEAD CHEDDAR & WHOLE WHEAT BISCUITS

Every good thing can be improved with cheese. At least that is my opinion, and no, that is not a paid endorsement for cheese. I just happen to love eating it, all kinds of it. I do believe that statement to be true, and biscuits are no exception. I recommend using a very flavorful aged cheddar here (we use a clothbound New York State one) so that the cheesy flavor does not become buried in the earthiness of the wheat. Something sharp, with a bit of a bite, is the type of juxtaposition you're looking for.

MAKES ABOUT 8 BISCUITS

1½ cups all-purpose flour

¼ cup whole wheat flour

¼ cup stone-ground cornmeal

1 tablespoon baking powder

½ teaspoon table salt

¼ teaspoon freshly ground black pepper

4 tablespoons (½ stick) cold unsalted butter, cut into pieces

¾ cup whole milk, plus 1 tablespoon for the egg wash

¾ cup (about 4 ounces) grated cheddar cheese

1 large egg yolk

1. Preheat the oven to 350°F.

2. In the bowl of a food processor, combine the flours, cornmeal, baking powder, salt, and pepper. Pulse to combine. Add the butter and pulse 4 or 5 times, until it is broken up into pea-sized pieces. Pour in half of the milk and pulse once. Add the remaining milk and the cheese, and pulse 3 times to combine. The dough should start to gather around the blade of the food processor.

3. Turn the dough out onto a lightly floured work surface. Flour your hands, and pat the dough into a 1-inch-thick circle. Using a 3-inch round biscuit cutter, cut out as many biscuits as you can. Place the biscuits on a parchment paper–lined baking sheet, spaced about an inch apart. Gently reshape the remaining dough, and once again cut out as many biscuits as possible. Add them to the baking sheet. (Any scraps that are left can be baked, but they will not have the same texture and lightness.)

4. In a small bowl, stir the egg yolk and the 1 tablespoon milk together with a fork. Brush the biscuits lightly with this egg wash.

5. Bake the biscuits for 10 minutes. Then rotate the baking sheet and bake for 8 to 10 more minutes, until both the tops and the bottoms of the biscuits are a rich golden color. Transfer the biscuits to a wire rack and let them cool for 5 minutes before serving.

HOMEMADE BUTTER

I have always been of the mind-set that if I am going to indulge by spreading butter on something I eat, it will be nothing but the best butter. So, like many others who share my philosophy, I have bought the finest and most expensive imported butters. I've tried Irish, French, and Italian butters and enjoyed them all. Little did I know that the best butter of all was sitting in a container of heavy cream in my refrigerator, waiting to be made. All it needed was a food processor and a few minutes of my time. I love it when something that seems so difficult is actually so easy.

MAKES 1 CUP

2 cups heavy cream, at room temperature

¼ teaspoon table salt

1. Pour the cream into a food processor, and turn on the processor. The cream will go through two distinct stages: First it will become whipped cream. Then continue processing until the cream separates. This can take 2 minutes or up to 5 or more minutes, depending on how warm the cream is.

2. When the cream separates, there will be yellow butter that balls up around the blade and buttermilk that looks like milky water. Strain the butter in a fine-mesh strainer, reserving the buttermilk for another use (such as for making Buttermilk Biscuits, page 127).

3. Next, wash out the butter: Return it to the food processor, add 1 cup of cold water, and process for 20 seconds. Strain this in the fine-mesh strainer, discarding the water. Repeat 3 more times, or until the water is almost clear after processing. This is an important part of the process because it separates out more of the buttermilk from the butter. Buttermilk spoils faster than butter, so this step keeps the butter fresher for a longer period.

4. Put the washed butter in a large bowl. Add the salt, and using a firm rubber spatula and a lot of elbow grease, work the salt into the butter. Buttermilk will continue to be released from the butter as you work it; drain it off as you go. Continue to work the butter for 3 to 5 minutes, draining off the excess water. Transfer the butter to an airtight container. The butter will keep in the refrigerator for 3 to 4 days, or in the freezer for up to 2 months.

HOMEMADE YOGURT

You may be thinking, "It's so much easier to buy yogurt than make my own, why would I go through the trouble?" Your point is a good one, but trust me when I say that it's one of those things you need to see for yourself. If you make it just once, you will need no further convincing, and I guarantee you'll begin turning your nose up at the store-bought version. The tang is stronger, the texture is creamier, and the flavor is fresher—so fresh that you may have a yearning to meet the cow that supplied the milk. It is so pure and good that I would liken it to feeding yourself big spoonfuls of good health.

MAKES ABOUT 32 OUNCES OF YOGURT

2 quarts whole milk

1 tablespoon plain whole-milk yogurt with active cultures

TIP: Note that for this recipe you will need a food-grade thermometer and a warm spot in your kitchen. Also, I try to use a nice-quality organic milk, possibly from a local dairy, for this recipe. The same for the yogurt, but these are not absolutely necessary.

1. Pour the milk into a large saucepan, and gradually warm it over medium heat, stirring frequently to prevent burning. When the temperature reaches 180°F, remove the pan from the heat and pour the milk into a large mixing bowl. Let it cool. When the milk has cooled to 110°F, stir in the yogurt.

2. Set the bowl in a warm place and do not disturb it for about 8 hours. (If you can set your oven to 100°F, this is perfect: put the bowl in the oven. Otherwise, if you have a gas oven, the pilot light will usually keep it warm enough; set the bowl on the area over the pilot light. Or you can set the bowl on top of a radiator, or even on a heating pad.)

3. After about 8 hours, scoop the yogurt into a cheesecloth-lined colander. Put the bowl in the refrigerator and strain the yogurt for 1 to 3 hours. The longer you strain it, the thicker it will be. Discard the whey that strains out of the yogurt. The yogurt can be stored in an airtight container in the refrigerator for up to 1 week.

"INSTANT" RICH HOT COCOA & HOMEMADE MARSHMALLOWS

We've all had various interpretations of hot cocoa, from the really watery ones that come from boxed mixes to super-duper rich ones that are amazingly good until a bellyache sets in after a few sips. This particular one straddles the line. It's decadent, but not overdone, and you're sure to thoroughly enjoy each and every sip. It's as easy as instant cocoa, minus any unpronounceable ingredients. The marshmallows are fun with a capital "F." They are one of the most squeezable foods on Earth . . . and after you're done playing with them, they are great to eat, too!

You will need between twenty-five and thirty small disposable paper cups for this recipe. Paper espresso cups or mini cupcake liners work very well. Even Dixie cups can do the trick.

MAKES ENOUGH FOR 25 TO 30 SERVINGS

2 cups semisweet chocolate chips

¼ teaspoon ground cinnamon

Hot milk, for serving

Homemade Marshmallows (recipe follows), for serving

1. In a small saucepan, heat ⅔ cup of water to a simmer. Pour the water into a heat-resistant bowl, and add the chocolate chips and cinnamon. Stir thoroughly until all of the chocolate has melted. Let the ganache cool for 20 minutes.

2. Pour 2 tablespoons of the ganache into each of 25 to 30 small paper cups. Transfer the cups to an airtight container, and put it in the refrigerator. Let cool completely. Sealed in an airtight container, these ganache cups will stay fresh for 2 weeks.

3. When you are ready for a cup of hot chocolate, fill your favorite mug halfway with hot milk, unwrap a ganache serving, and drop it into the mug. Stir thoroughly until the ganache has melted. Serve with a homemade marshmallow.

VARIATIONS

If you're feeling sassy, either the chocolate or the marshmallows can be flavored with cinnamon or mint.

HOMEMADE MARSHMALLOWS

MAKES 24 MARSHMALLOWS

3 envelopes unflavored gelatin

2 cups sugar

¾ cup light corn syrup

½ teaspoon salt

2 teaspoons vanilla extract

About 1 cup confectioners' sugar

Coat a 9 × 13-inch baking pan with cooking spray, line the bottom with parchment paper, and spray the parchment paper also.

Pour ½ cup of cold water into the bowl of an electric mixer fitted with the whisk attachment. Sprinkle the gelatin over the surface of the water, and let it sit and absorb the water while you prepare the other ingredients.

In a heavy-bottomed saucepan set over medium heat, combine the sugar, corn syrup, salt, and ½ cup of water. Stir until the sugar has dissolved. Bring the mixture up to a boil, cover the pan with a tight-fitting lid, and boil for 5 minutes. Remove the lid and do not stir the syrup any more as it is heating.

Being careful to agitate the pot as little as possible, attach a candy thermometer to the side of the pan. Continue to boil the syrup until it reaches 240°F. Be attentive toward the end because you do not want to overheat it.

When the syrup reaches 240°F, carefully remove the pan from the heat. Turn the electric mixer on low speed, and carefully pour the hot syrup into the bowl of gelatin. Increase the speed to high, and beat for 8 minutes. With the machine still running on high speed, add the vanilla. Continue whipping as the marshmallow becomes light and fluffy. After 5 to 7 minutes, the mixture will be stiff and lukewarm. Turn the mixer off and carefully scrape the marshmallow into the prepared baking pan. Using a spatula that has been sprayed with cooking spray, smooth the top of the marshmallow. Let it cool, uncovered, at room temperature for at least 5 hours.

To cut the marshmallows, sprinkle a generous amount of confectioners' sugar on a cutting board. Turn the marshmallow out of the pan onto the cutting board. Sprinkle the top and sides with more confectioners' sugar. Spray a large chef's knife with cooking spray, and carefully cut the marshmallows into 2-inch cubes. This is a very sticky business! Use plenty of confectioners' sugar on your hands and on the marshmallows to help you fight the stickiness. The marshmallows will keep in an airtight container at room temperature for 5 to 6 days.

Family Recipes

fumusa family party, 1957, bushwick, brooklyn

NANA COOKIES

As they say, it's all in the name—but that's especially true when the name is Nana. I'm not sure how these humble little piped cookies earned the honor of being named after my grandmother, but I think it's because she was the only person in the entire world (at least my world) who made them. Now that she's no longer here to make them, Aunt Tina does, but it just wouldn't have been right to change the name. They are a staple at every family gathering and have been for as long as I can remember. I imagine many generations to come will say the same thing.

They are deceiving, these cookies, because they are made from a very simple dough, the only flavoring being ground cloves. But don't be fooled. They are addictive and loved by everyone who tries them—after a dunk in their coffee, of course!

MAKES 36 COOKIES

2½ cups all-purpose flour

1 tablespoon baking powder

½ teaspoon ground cloves

¼ teaspoon salt

6 tablespoons solid vegetable shortening, at room temperature

4 tablespoons (½ stick) unsalted butter, at room temperature

¾ cup sugar

1 large egg

1 large egg yolk

¼ cup whole milk

1. Preheat the oven to 350°F.

2. In a medium bowl, whisk together the flour, baking powder, cloves, and salt.

3. In the bowl of an electric mixer fitted with the paddle attachment, beat together the shortening, butter, and sugar on medium speed until the mixture is light yellow and fluffy, about 3 minutes. Scrape down the sides of the bowl with a rubber spatula. Add the egg and egg yolk, and beat for 1 minute. Scrape down the bowl again.

4. With the mixer running on low speed, mix in a third of the flour mixture and about a third of the milk. Scrape down the bowl. Add another third of the flour mixture and another third of the milk. Add the remaining flour mixture and only enough of the milk to make a smooth dough. It should not be too sticky.

5. Using a large pastry bag fitted with a star tip, pipe 1½-inch-long cookies onto a parchment paper–lined baking sheet, spacing them 1 inch apart. Bake for 15 minutes until the cookies take on a little golden color along the edge. Transfer the cookies to a wire rack and let them cool completely.

CONNIE'S MERINGUES

There are three dishes that Dave's grandmother (whom everyone, including her grandchildren, referred to as "Connie") was known for: beef stew, soft-boiled eggs, and meringues. The meringues are the things that Dave remembers most vividly because they were her "special occasion" dessert. Connie typically made these simple, crunchy sweets at Thanksgiving or Christmas, so they're attached to memories of family gatherings. The recipe is so easy that we hope you'll enjoy them year-round. We think that they're especially good when topped with some fresh summer fruit or our stewed fruit (page 120).

MAKES 36 MERINGUES

3 large egg whites

1 teaspoon vanilla extract

¼ teaspoon table salt

¼ teaspoon cream of tartar

¾ cup sugar

1. Preheat the oven to 200°F. Line a baking sheet with parchment paper.

2. In the bowl of an electric mixer fitted with the whisk attachment, beat the egg whites for 2 minutes on medium speed. Add the vanilla, salt, and cream of tartar. Increase the mixer speed to high and beat for 30 seconds. With the mixer running on high speed, add the sugar, about 1 tablespoon at a time, and continue to beat until stiff peaks form, about 2 minutes.

3. Using two large spoons, scoop out some batter and form it into an oval shape by scooping the batter back and forth between the spoons. Gently place it on a parchment paper–lined baking sheet. Repeat, spacing the meringues an inch apart.

4. Bake for 1½ to 2 hours, until the meringues are crisp and dry. Transfer them to a wire rack to cool. The meringues will keep in an airtight container at room temperature for 3 to 4 days.

AUNT TINA'S PUMPKIN CHOCOLATE CHIP COOKIES

Most of the desserts described in this chapter have been in my or Dave's family for generations. This is the one exception. My mom's sister, Aunt Tina, made these one year to bring to my birthday celebration, and they quickly became a part of just about every subsequent gathering. Usually she makes them as the kids' dessert, but truth be told, it's the adults who can't keep their hands off them.

MAKES 36 COOKIES

2 cups all-purpose flour

1 teaspoon baking powder

1/2 teaspoon baking soda

1/2 teaspoon table salt

1 cup (2 sticks) unsalted butter, at room temperature

1 cup sugar

1 large egg

1 teaspoon vanilla extract

1 cup canned pumpkin puree

2 cups semisweet chocolate chips

1. In a medium bowl, whisk together the flour, baking powder, baking soda, and salt.

2. In the bowl of an electric mixer fitted with the paddle attachment, beat together the butter and sugar on medium speed until the mixture is light yellow and fluffy, about 3 minutes. Scrape down the sides of the bowl with a rubber spatula.

3. With the mixer running on low speed, add the egg and vanilla and mix for 30 seconds, until fully combined. Scrape down the bowl. Add the pumpkin puree and mix on medium speed for 30 seconds. Scrape down the bowl thoroughly. With the mixer running on low speed, add the flour mixture and mix for 10 seconds. Take the bowl off the mixer, add the chocolate chips, and finish mixing the dough with a rubber spatula. Cover the bowl with plastic wrap and chill the dough in the refrigerator for at least 1 hour, or preferably overnight.

4. Preheat the oven to 350°F.

5. Using a small cookie scoop, scoop small rounds of dough—about 1½ tablespoons in size—onto a parchment paper–lined baking sheet, spacing them 2 inches apart. The dough will be very sticky.

6. Bake the cookies for 7 minutes. Rotate the baking sheet and bake for 7 more minutes, or until the cookies are a dark golden color around the edges. Let the cookies cool for about 10 minutes on the baking sheet. Transfer them to a wire rack and let them cool completely.

FIG COOKIES

Every December, my mom and Aunt Tina head up the annual operation of baking mounds of fig cookies, effortlessly showing the next generation (my sisters and me) how to perfectly score the cookies with a razor blade (the desired result is a lovely fanlike pattern in the baked cookie). After working hard to make dozens of cookies, we each take home our ration and do our best to make it last as long as possible, knowing there will be no more fig cookies for quite some time. This makes us very good at self-control and very bad at sharing.

Because I actually want people to make these delicious fig-filled gems, I am offering an adaptation of the original method. Cutting the designs with razor blades takes lots of practice and is best learned from experts. Truth be told, my sisters' and mine pale in comparison to the beauties Aunt Tina and my mom make.

Have patience as you get started, because your first few cookies might be a bit messy or not as pretty as you'd like. They take some practice, but once you get it down, you just might feel compelled to start a family tradition of your own.

MAKES 40 COOKIES

FILLING

1¼ pounds dried figs

Peeled zest of 1 orange

1 cup blanched almonds, toasted and chopped

½ cup orange marmalade

½ cup mini semisweet chocolate chips

¼ cup sugar

1 teaspoon Dutch-processed cocoa powder

¼ teaspoon ground cloves

¼ teaspoon ground cinnamon

1. To make the filling, combine the figs and the orange zest in a food processor, and process for 1 minute, until thoroughly chopped. Transfer the fig mixture to a large bowl. Add the almonds, marmalade, chocolate chips, sugar, cocoa powder, cloves, and cinnamon, and mix thoroughly. If the mixture is too stiff, add warm water, a teaspoon at a time, until the mixture is a thick paste.

2. To make the dough, combine the flour, sugar, and baking powder in the bowl of an electric mixer fitted with the paddle attachment. Mix on low speed to combine. With the mixer running on low speed, add the shortening, 1 tablespoon at a time, and mix until well combined. Then add water, 1 teaspoon at a time, until the dough begins to ball around the paddle (you may need to add up to 1 cup of water). Transfer the dough to a lightly floured work surface, and knead it for 2 to 3 minutes, until it is smooth. Cover the dough with a moist cloth.

3. Preheat the oven to 350°F.

(recipe continues)

4. To make the cookies, lightly flour a work surface. Break off small pieces of the dough, and using your hands, roll them into logs that are 1 inch thick and 6 inches long. (Keep any dough that you are not using covered by the damp cloth.) Cut each log into 1-inch-thick coins. Using a rolling pin, roll out each coin until it is about ⅛-inch thick. Place about 1 teaspoon of the fig filling in the center of each round of dough. Using your fingers, bring two sides of the round up and pinch them over the filling, sealing the edge of the dough. Turn the cookie over so the seam is on the bottom, and shape the cookie into an almond shape. Repeat until you have used all of the filling and dough.

5. Transfer the cookies to a parchment paper–lined baking sheet, spacing them 1 inch apart. With a very sharp paring knife (or a razor blade, if you want to be authentic), slice vents in the side or in the top of each cookie.

6. Bake for 10 minutes. Then rotate the baking sheet and bake for another 8 to 10 minutes, until the cookies are a very light golden color. Transfer the cookies to a wire rack and let cool completely.

7. Store the cookies in an airtight container and bring them to me at the shop. I love these cookies!

PIZZELLE

My dad's parents, Nanny and Poppy, lived in the next town over from us. At their house on Saxon Drive my sisters, cousins, and I played endless games of hide-and-seek, watched Fourth of July fireworks, and learned a couple of tunes on Poppy's organ. I have such fond memories of that house, but not many involve food. There was always an Entenmann's crumb cake and some coffee ice cream around the house, but big home-cooked feasts were not Nanny's cup of tea.

That being said, these pizzelle were one of her few specialties. They are melt-in-your-mouth wafers, so light that a strong breeze could reduce them to crumbs. Their appeal lies in that delicate quality, which Nanny's eleven grandchildren could attest to. Keeping twenty-two little hands off of the pizzelle required far more effort than actually making them did. A pizzelle iron (similar to a waffle iron) is required for these, but I am certain you will not regret the investment.

MAKES 30 PIZELLE

3 large eggs

1 cup sugar

2 teaspoons vanilla extract

1 teaspoon anise liqueur or anise flavoring

1 teaspoon baking powder

1/2 cup canola oil

1 1/2 cups all-purpose flour

1. In the bowl of an electric mixer fitted with the paddle attachment, beat together the eggs and sugar for 1 minute on medium speed. Add the vanilla, anise liqueur, and baking powder. Mix to combine. With the mixer running on medium speed, drizzle in the oil. Remove the bowl from the mixer, add the flour, and fold it in with a rubber spatula. Let the batter rest for 15 minutes while you heat up the pizzelle iron.

2. Preheat the pizzelle iron until it is very hot. Spoon about 1 tablespoon of the batter onto the mold. (Experiment with your iron to see how much batter is needed to make a perfect pizzelle.) Cook the pizzelle for about 1 minute, or until it is golden brown. Then transfer it to a wire rack to cool. Repeat with the remaining batter. The pizzelle will keep in an airtight container at room temperature for 5 to 6 days.

RICOTTA-FILLED TURNOVERS

One glance at this dessert and I am transported to my Nana's upstairs kitchen (yes, like every good Italian, she had two in her small Queens apartment) and I am about nine. She is frying these up and allowing me to snatch a couple and gobble them down while they are warm. The pastry is golden and crunchy and the sweet ricotta filling is creamy. As I tell the story, I can close my eyes and swear that I can taste them.

Cassateddi were always a special-occasion dessert, and if you attempt making them, you'll soon realize why. They are definitely a bit labor-intensive and messy (due to the frying), but worth every ounce of effort and dish soap. They resemble an empanada with their flaky outer crust, but are filled with either lemon-scented or chocolate-studded sweet ricotta.

MAKES 20 TURNOVERS

1 pound ricotta

DOUGH
4 cups all-purpose flour

½ cup sugar

10 tablespoons solid vegetable shortening

2 tablespoons sweet white wine

FILLINGS
¾ cup sugar

½ teaspoon vanilla extract

½ cup semisweet chocolate chips

Grated zest of 2 lemons

Vegetable oil, for frying

1. Put the ricotta in a cheesecloth-lined colander (coffee filters work as well). Set the colander in a larger bowl and cover it with plastic wrap. Let the ricotta drain overnight in the refrigerator to remove most of the water. (If you are using fresh ricotta, then it is probably dry enough as it is.)

2. To make the dough, combine the flour and the sugar in the bowl of an electric mixer fitted with the paddle attachment, and mix on low speed. With the mixer running on low speed, add the shortening 1 tablespoon at a time. Continue mixing on low speed until combined. With the machine still running on low speed, drizzle in 1 tablespoon of the white wine. Continue to add more wine, 1 teaspoon at a time, until the dough begins to form a ball. Take the dough out of the mixing bowl and knead on a lightly floured surface for 2 to 3 minutes until it is smooth. Cover the dough with a moist cloth and let it rest for 20 minutes.

3. To make the fillings, mix together the drained ricotta, sugar, and vanilla in a large bowl. Divide the mixture between two mixing bowls. Add the chocolate chips to one bowl and mix well. Add the lemon zest to the other bowl and mix well.

4. To make the turnovers, lightly flour a work surface. Pinch off a few golf-ball-sized pieces of dough, and roll them into balls between the

palms of your hands. (Keep the remaining dough covered with the cloth to keep it fresh.) Using a rolling pin, roll each ball of dough into a thin oval shape. Put a small dollop of the chocolate filling in the center of the oval. Wet the edges of the dough with a little bit of water, fold the dough over the filling, and pinch the edges to seal them. Repeat, using all the dough and both fillings.

5. In a deep pot, heat 2 inches of oil to 375°F.

6. Before you fry the turnovers, reseal the edges of the turnovers. Pinch them well, because if the filling spills out in the pot of oil, it will make a big mess. Work in batches so that you do not crowd the pot. Carefully drop the turnovers into the hot oil and cook for about 1 minute, turning them once with a slotted spoon, until they turn a lovely golden color. Remove them from the oil and let them drain on paper towels. Let the cassateddi cool for 5 minutes before serving.

SICILIAN DOUGHNUT HOLES

If you are able to refrain from eating these while making them, congratulations are in order. Sfinge are basically Sicilian doughnut holes, and whenever possible, they should be enjoyed warm, drizzled with honey. Now that Nanny is not here to make them, Aunt Diane has become the designated sfinge maker. I do not envy her that title because, as our family grows, so must her bowl of sfinge, and that is quite an undertaking since they require good old-fashioned deep frying.

Hopefully your family is not offended by double-dipping, because proper sfinge consumption requires sopping up more of the warm honey from the bottom of the bowl for your second bite—that is, if there is a second bite!

MAKES 40

1 pound ricotta

1 cup all-purpose flour

1 teaspoon baking powder

6 large eggs

½ cup sugar

2 teaspoons vanilla extract

Vegetable oil, for frying

Honey, for serving

1. Put the ricotta in a cheesecloth-lined colander (coffee filters work as well). Set the colander in a larger bowl and cover it with plastic wrap. Let the ricotta drain overnight in the refrigerator to remove most of the water. (If you are using fresh ricotta, then it is probably dry enough as it is.)

2. In a medium bowl, whisk together the flour and baking powder.

3. In the bowl of an electric mixer fitted with the paddle attachment, beat together the eggs, sugar, and vanilla on medium speed for 2 minutes. Scrape down the sides of the bowl. With the mixer running on low speed, add a third of the flour mixture and then half of the ricotta. Mix for 10 seconds. Briefly scrape down the bowl and the paddle. With the mixer running on low speed, add another third of the flour mixture and all the remaining ricotta. Mix for 10 seconds. Scrape down the bowl and paddle. Remove the bowl from the mixer, add the rest of the flour mixture, and mix with a rubber spatula until fully combined.

4. In a deep pot, heat 2 inches of vegetable oil to 375°F. Carefully drop tablespoon-sized scoops of the batter into the hot oil and cook for 2 minutes, turning them with a slotted spoon, until they are golden. Remove the sfinge from the oil and let them drain on paper towels.

5. To serve, drizzle honey over the sfinge.

My Pizz

3 eggs beaten
1 cup sugar (scant) (oleg)
1 st melted butter
...flour
...powder
...lla
...e
...d too thick

Sfenge's Millie)
Polly O-
1 lb ricotta (whole milk)
1 cup flour
6 eggs
1 tbls sugar
1 tbls Baking Powder
1 tea vanilla (add more)

Mix eggs beat adding
sugar - B.P. add
vanilla mix well alterna-
ting flour and ricotta
until well blended -
Drop into hot oil
a teaspoonful
sure oil
enough.

...full tea...
Soften butte...
adding sugar...
very well, as...
the add 1 cup...
very until all...
are very well...
Put dough into...
pating well into...
a little water to...
on top of dough for...
Bake 350 for 1/2...
golden brown -

SICILIAN FROZEN TRIFLE

This is a signature Sicilian dessert, though I strangely have no memory of eating it as a kid. The recipe comes from my mom and has become one of my favorites. It serves well as an adult birthday cake because it involves a cakey element (think Sicilian pound cake) and a creamy element (think cannoli cream). That being said, I hope that you don't save it for birthdays only. Besides being delicious, this dessert is convenient because it is frozen once it is assembled. You can leave it in your freezer (wrapped in plastic) for several days. That attribute comes in handy if you are anything like my mom, who entertains many people often.

MAKES ONE 9 X 5-INCH LOAF CAKE

CAKE
1 cup cake flour

1 teaspoon baking powder

1/2 teaspoon salt

1/4 cup whole milk

1 teaspoon vanilla extract

8 tablespoons (1 stick) unsalted butter, at room temperature

3/4 cup sugar

2 large eggs

Grated zest of 1 orange

RICOTTA FILLING
2 cups fresh ricotta (see Tip)

1 cup sugar

Grated zest of 1 orange

1 teaspoon vanilla extract

1/2 cup mini chocolate chips

1. To make the cake, preheat the oven to 350°F. Spray a 9 × 5-inch loaf pan with cooking spray and dust it with flour, knocking out any excess.

2. In a medium bowl, whisk together the cake flour, baking soda, and salt.

3. In a small bowl, combine the milk and vanilla.

4. In the bowl of an electric mixer fitted with the paddle attachment, beat together the butter and sugar on medium speed until the mixture is light yellow and fluffy, about 3 minutes. Scrape down the sides of the bowl with a rubber spatula. Add the eggs one at a time, mixing well after each addition; and then add the orange zest. Mix on medium speed for 1 minute. With the mixer running on low speed, mix in a third of the flour mixture and half of the milk mixture. Scrape down the bowl. Add another third of the flour mixture and all the remaining milk mixture. Remove the bowl from the mixer, and using a rubber spatula, fold in the remaining flour mixture until all of the ingredients are fully incorporated.

5. Pour the batter into the prepared loaf pan and bake for 25 minutes. Rotate the pan and bake for 20 more minutes, or until a cake tester inserted in the center of the cake comes out clean. Remove the pan from the oven and let the cake cool in the pan for 20 minutes. Then turn the cake out onto a wire rack and let it cool completely.

(recipe continues)

WHIPPED CREAM

2 cups heavy cream

¼ teaspoon almond extract

¼ cup confectioners' sugar

TIP: Store-bought regular ricotta has more water in it than fresh, so you'll need to drain it before making the filling. Put the ricotta in a cheesecloth-lined colander (coffee filters work as well), set the colander into a larger bowl, and cover it with plastic wrap. Let the ricotta drain overnight in the refrigerator to remove most of the water.

6. To make the ricotta filling, combine the ricotta and sugar in the bowl of an electric mixer fitted with the paddle attachment. Beat on medium speed for 1 minute, until soft. Add the orange zest and the vanilla, and mix for 30 seconds. Scrape down the bowl and the paddle. On low speed, add the chocolate chips and mix for just 5 seconds to incorporate.

7. To make the whipped cream, combine the cream and the almond extract in the clean bowl of the electric mixer fitted with the whisk attachment, and whip for 30 seconds on medium speed. Raise the speed to high and whip for 1 more minute. Reduce the speed to medium and gradually add the confectioners' sugar. Whip on high speed for 3 to 5 minutes, until the whipped cream is firm.

8. To assemble the trifle, slice the cake horizontally into 3 layers. Place the bottom (widest) layer on a serving plate. Spread a ½-inch-thick layer of the ricotta filling over the cake layer. Repeat for the next 2 layers, but do not put ricotta on top of the final cake layer. Cover the entire cake with the whipped cream. Transfer the cake to the freezer and freeze for at least 2 hours, or up to 8 hours.

MILK PIE

I will never forget sharing my first meal with the Crofton family. I felt comfortable almost immediately—until dessert came out and someone offered me a piece of milk pie. Certainly the expression on my face said it all. "Milk what?" Perhaps a glass of milk with my pie? No, I had heard right. Milk pie. But I felt like an outsider for only a moment, as I quickly came to love and understand this most simple of pies. Consisting of a few basic ingredients, it was perfected by Dave's aunt Peggy. The milky-custardy flavor is so pure that I consider it to be Crofton comfort food.

MAKES ONE 9-INCH PIE

CRUST

1⅓ cups all-purpose flour

¼ teaspoon table salt

⅓ cup canola oil

3 tablespoons whole milk, plus more if needed

FILLING

⅓ cup all-purpose flour

¾ cup sugar

⅛ teaspoon table salt

⅛ teaspoon baking powder

2 cups half-and-half

1 teaspoon cold unsalted butter, cut into pieces

⅛ teaspoon ground cinnamon

Pinch of ground mace

1. To make the crust, whisk together the flour and salt in a large bowl.

2. In a separate bowl, mix the oil and milk with a fork. Using a rubber spatula, stir the milk mixture into the flour mixture until the dough forms a ball. If the dough is too dry, add a few drops of milk. In the mixing bowl, knead the dough by hand for 1 minute.

3. Place a sheet of parchment paper on a flat work surface, put the dough on the parchment, and top it with a second sheet of parchment. Roll the dough out to form an 11-inch round. Carefully transfer the dough to a 9-inch pie dish, making sure that the edge of the pie is smooth and even. Place the pie dish on a baking sheet.

4. Preheat the oven to 400°F.

5. To make the filling, whisk together the flour, sugar, salt, and baking powder in a medium bowl. Put the mixture into the pie shell, and using your fingertips, make small furrows. Pour in the half-and-half. Scatter the butter pieces over the top, and sprinkle with the cinnamon and mace.

6. Bake the pie for 10 minutes. Reduce the oven temperature to 325°F and bake, rotating the pan halfway through, for 50 minutes, until the filling is a light golden color and jiggles slightly when you jostle the baking sheet. If the pie looks too liquid, bake it for an additional 10 minutes or more. Transfer the pie dish to a wire rack and let the pie cool completely. Serve at room temperature.

RICOTTA CHEESECAKE
with Candied Fruit

When I was growing up, whenever cheesecake came up in conversation it was necessary to identify what style you meant: American or Italian. We took this distinction almost as seriously as the difference between brown (American) coffee and black (espresso).

The differences between this cheesecake and the more traditional type are great. To start, this version has a curdy texture from the ricotta which I think is really fabulous. It also incorporates candied fruit, which I know is not for everyone, but I think it gives this cake real personality. Dave decided to make his own using lemon and orange zest (see page 70), a recipe that may change your mind about candied fruit forever. Another differentiating factor here is the crust, which is essentially a pie crust bottom and stands up to the weight of this cheesecake better. But to me, the most important difference is that this is the one I have a personal connection to because it's the one Nana made.

MAKES ONE 9-INCH
CAKE

2 lemons

2 navel oranges

3 cups plus 3 tablespoons sugar

1 cup all-purpose flour

Pinch of table salt

6 tablespoons (¾ stick) cold unsalted butter, cut into pieces

3 pounds fresh ricotta (see Tip, page 150)

8 large eggs, separated

1 teaspoon vanilla extract

Grated zest of 1 lemon

½ cup all-purpose flour

½ cup heavy cream

1. Using a citrus zester (you can use a vegetable peeler, but make sure you cut very thin strips of zest without much rind), make long, thin strips of zest from the oranges. Put the zest in a small saucepan, cover with water, and bring to a boil over high heat. Drain off the water and repeat the boiling and draining process two more times. Set the drained zest aside. In a clean saucepan, bring 1 cup of water and 1 cup of the sugar to a boil. Stir in the zest. Simmer for 4 minutes, remove the pan from the heat, and let cool. Drain the fruit from the syrup and set aside.

2. Preheat the oven to 350°F. Prepare a 9-inch springform pan by coating it with cooking spray.

3. In the bowl of an electric mixer fitted with the paddle attachment, combine the flour, 3 tablespoons of the sugar, and salt. With the machine running on low speed, gradually add the pieces of butter. Increase speed to medium low and mix for 3 to 5 more minutes until the mixture begins to form small crumbs.

4. Turn dough out into the prepared pan and, using your fingers, press the dough into the bottom of the pan, making sure that the dough is

fairly even in thickness. Prick the crust all over with the tines of a fork. Refrigerate the dough for 20 minutes.

5. Bake the crust for 5 minutes. Rotate the pan and bake for 5 more minutes. Transfer the pan to a wire rack and let the crust cool completely. Increase the oven temperature to 425°F.

6. In the bowl of an electric mixer fitted with the paddle attachment, beat the ricotta for 30 seconds on medium speed to soften it. With the mixer running on low speed, add the candied zest and 1½ cups of the sugar and the egg yolks, vanilla, and lemon zest. Scrape down the sides of the bowl with a rubber spatula. Add the flour and mix on low speed for only 10 seconds. Scrape down the bowl again. Transfer the mixture to a large bowl.

7. In the clean bowl of the electric mixer fitted with the whisk attachment, whip the egg whites on medium speed for 30 seconds. Reduce the speed to medium-low and slowly add the remaining ½ cup sugar. Then raise the speed to high and whip the egg whites until they form stiff peaks, about 2 minutes. Transfer the egg whites to a large bowl.

8. In the clean bowl of the electric mixer fitted with the clean whisk attachment, whip the heavy cream on medium speed for 30 seconds. Increase the speed to high and continue to mix until the cream forms stiff peaks. Gently fold the whipped cream into the egg whites. Then gently fold the egg white mixture into the ricotta mixture.

9. Put the springform pan on a baking sheet, and pour the filling into the pan. Bake for 10 minutes. Then reduce the oven temperature to 300°F, and bake for 1 hour, or until the cake is a rich golden color and a cake tester inserted in the center of the cake comes out clean.

10. Remove the pan from the oven and let it cool for 10 minutes. Then run a sharp knife around the edge of the cake to loosen it from the sides of the pan. Let the cake cool completely before you release the spring.

PACKAGING

The manner in which we package our gift boxes of tea cookies is something that I'm quite proud of. Each variety is wrapped in its own cellophane sleeve, tied closed on either end with satin ribbon, and placed in a rectangular kraft box. Then a vintage family photo, a decorative paper band, and a ribbon are added as the final pretty touches. These elements are uniquely ours and have made our gift boxes very identifiable. If you've been to our shop or visited our web site, it's quite apparent that aesthetics are paramount to everything—except flavor and customer service. I have no doubt that I inherited this philosophy and skill from my mom. She is that person who would never dream of placing a plastic container or a cooking pot on the table. Instead, even leftovers were transferred to the prettiest of serving pieces and given proper respect. As you would guess, when she took the time to make a delicious dessert, she also took the time to artfully arrange it on a lovely tray or dish.

I have embraced that way of doing things and taken it a step further. Just set me loose in a paper store and you'll see what I mean. When I am surrounded by decorative papers, beautiful ribbons, pretty hang tags, and such, I become giddy just thinking about the packaging possibilities. Sometimes even the most common materials, like twine or Mason jars, can be used creatively to transform the sweets I make into pretty gifts.

An extra ounce of effort usually goes a long way in making a gift recipient feel really special. And how great is it to see how special they feel once they bite into the delicious treats you've made for them!

HERE ARE JUST A FEW IDEAS TO SPARK YOUR CREATIVE JUICES.

BAKEWARE: A vintage baking vessel such as a loaf, cupcake, or Bundt pan serves a dual purpose: getting your home-baked sweets into the hands of the lucky recipient, who can then use it to bake her own sweets. Line the pan with a pretty piece of linen and add a thoughtful touch by including the recipe.

JARS: You can find some fantastic old jars that would be the perfect home for some freshly baked cookies. Tie some baker's twine or ribbon around the neck, and add a tag with a message. Baker's twine is available in all sorts of colors these days, not just red, so take your pick.

PAPER: Even a simple bakery box can be gussied up with the simple addition of a band of decorative paper. Choose a style that reflects the personality of the person you're giving it to, the sweets inside the box, or the particular occasion. I usually cut the paper about half as wide as the box and adhere it with double-sided stick tape either in the center or on the left side.

RESOURCES: Some of my favorite places to find interesting packaging elements are Etsy (www.etsy.com) for ribbons, twine, and hang tags; New York Central Art Supply (www.nycentralart.com) for a great array of decorative papers; and flea markets and eBay (www.eBay.com) for vintage baking pans and jars.

ACKNOWLEDGMENTS

OUR HEARTFELT THANKS TO . . .

- Our editor, Ashley Phillips, who patiently guided us, as first-time authors, through the book-writing process. We are grateful to her for always recognizing how personal these stories and recipes are to us.

- Everyone at Clarkson Potter, especially Lauren Shakely, Doris Cooper, Rica Allannic, Marysarah Quinn, Rae Ann Spitzenberger, Rachelle Mandik, and Alexis Mentor for believing we had a story worth telling and helping us to tell it.

- Iain Bagwell and Amy Wilson, for attending to every detail while photographing and styling this book. The beautiful book we envisioned has become a reality.

- Our One Girl Cookies family, for treating our business as their own, for holding down the fort and ensuring our customers were well taken care of while we were busy writing a book. You are a joy to work with.

- Our loyal customers and community, without whom there would be no One Girl Cookies. We are proud to call you neighbors and friends.

- Our fellow Brooklyn entrepreneurs, who inspire and support us.

- Steve Sotland, who gave us our first break by sharing his kitchen with us when One Girl was ready to grow and showered us with useful business advice.

- All of the friends and strangers who kindly tested our recipes.

- Judy, Trevor, Andrea, and Brenda for sharing their expertise with us.

- Each and every one of our friends and extended family who have been our enthusiastic cheerleaders from day one.

FROM DAWN . . .

- Tom, for allowing me to run a cookie company from his bedroom and tolerating an apartment filled with bakery boxes and crumbs.

- My grandmothers and all of the women in my family who have come before me. I have you to thank for passing on the recipes, traditions, and joys of the kitchen through the generations.

- Aunt Tina, for keeping those family recipes alive and for baking thousands of Nana and fig cookies.

- Jen, Nicole, and Danielle, for sharing with me a childhood filled with the memories and experiences I have written about. And for not telling me I was completely crazy, even if you thought I was.

- My parents, who taught me I could do anything I put my mind to. Your pride in me was the encouragement I needed during those times of doubt.

- Dave, my partner in life and cookies. I will always laugh at your jokes. Please keep them coming.

FROM DAVE . . .

- Dawn, for making my life as full and rich as I could ever imagine.

- My mom, for her endless supply of love and support throughout every aspect of my life.

- My dad, for always having time to listen to my ideas and sharing his wisdom.

- Dee, whose potato salad, chocolate chip cookies, and love made me the man I am today.

- The rest of my family, for your patience, guidance, and help with cookie tasting.

INDEX